DEEP MENDE

RELIGIOUS INTERACTIONS IN A CHANGING
AFRICAN RURAL SOCIETY

STUDIES ON RELIGION
IN AFRICA

SUPPLEMENTS TO THE JOURNAL OF RELIGION IN AFRICA

IV

LEIDEN
E. J. BRILL
1976

DEEP MENDE

RELIGIOUS INTERACTIONS IN A CHANGING AFRICAN RURAL SOCIETY

BY

DARRELL REECK

LEIDEN
E. J. BRILL
1976

ISBN 90 04 04769 7

CONTENTS

CONTENTS

PREFACE

My interest in Sierra Leone arose as a result of my childhood and youth activity in The United Methodist (then the Evangelical United Brethren) Church, through which the names of African and missionary leaders of the Sierra Leone Conference became familiar to me. After graduation from college, I traveled in West Africa for about three months in 1960-1961 and awakened to the intricacies and depth of African culture. This awareness was heightened in courses at Evangelical Theological Seminary under the late Wilbur Harr, Professor of Christian Missions. In 1966, I enrolled in the doctoral program in Social Ethics and Sociology of Religion at Boston University, and was very pleased to find that courses in the social sciences from the African Studies Center were applicable to the degree requirements in social ethics.

It seemed both interesting and logical to pursue some problem in African social history for a dissertation topic, and I was encouraged to do so by advisors. Paul K. Deats, Jr., Professor of Social Ethics, and Daniel F. McCall, Professor of Anthropology, served in that order as first and second readers of my dissertation, which was approved in 1970 under the title, "A Socio-Historical Analysis of Modernization and Related Mission Influences in Two Chiefdoms in West Africa, 1875-1940."

The Institute of African Studies at Fourah Bay College, the University of Sierra Leone, received me as a Visiting Research Fellow for a year of field study during 1968-1969. Principal Harry Sawyerr of Fourah Bay College was instrumental in arranging facilities and hospitality. J. K. Edowu Hyde, Esq., Secretary of the Institute of African Studies, provided valuable assistance in arranging introductions and in many other details. Michael Jolliffe, Esq., Librarian at Fourah Bay College and Acting Government Archivist, provided study space and orientation to the Sierra Leone Government Archives. S. J. A. Nelson, Esq., Chief Cartographer Technician of the Geography Department, prepared the original of the detail map of Sierra Leone included with the text. Some of my fellow researchers at the institute were very helpful in orienting me to sources and issues, and in giving me impetus to get on with the work.

Missionaries, pastors and members of The United Methodist Church in Sierra Leone, especially the Rev. Clyde Galow, Field Representative of the Board of Missions, were unfailing in providing access to rare printed materials and in making many practical arrangements. Dr. John Ness, Jr., Executive Secretary of the Commission on Archives and History of The United Methodist Church, was a source of encouragement and of archival assistance.

I wish to emphasize my appreciation of my informants and other interested parties, including Daniel Sam of Taiama, C. Myers of Rotifunk, and S. H. Thomas of Taiama (my primary translators), hundreds of villagers, chiefs, church workers, traders, school teachers and others. They gave much to this study — oral information, directions along bush paths, food, friendship and humor — and allowed me to merge into the richness of their lives for a time.

Those who were closest to me during the entire period, particularly my wife, Lucille, but also other relatives, bore many of the practical and mundane burdens willingly. I am pleased to be able to dedicate the book to Lucille.

All of the foregoing assisted with my dissertation work. Chapters two, three and four of the present text are substantial revisions of parts of the dissertation, and my colleagues in the departments of religion and sociology at the University of Puget Sound encouraged me with the rewriting. Mrs. Phoebe Miller, Associate Professor of Anthropology, was especially helpful in editorial and conceptual suggestions for chapter four. Chapter five is based on the research done for the dissertation, but was written later. Chapters one and six are freshly conceived and written.

The relationship between this book and my dissertation should be specified a bit more. The dissertation is longer; the book omits much of the technical discussion of modernization theory and some empirical data. Readers interested in that sort of detail should read the dissertation, available from University Microfilms, Ann Arbor, Michigan. The book emphasizes an interpretation growing out of the dissertation, namely, the continuing vitality and strength of African traditional culture and religion.

Research and writing goes slowly and takes funds. The receipt of a Rockefeller Doctoral Dissertation Year Fellowship, awarded by the Fund for Theological Education, Princeton, New Jersey, was a major factor in making the year in Sierra Leone possible. The Oral Data Committee of the African Studies Association made a grant in aid to assist with the preparation of the manuscripts of my interviews.[1] Additional grants from the Faculty Research Committee of the University of Puget Sound were helpful in meeting expenses connected with the preparation and publication of the book manuscript.

To the foregoing persons and institutions I offer hearty thanks. I hope that their participation in the process will be rewarded. They all share credit for any success, though responsibility for error is mine alone. I wish to thank the editors of *Geneva-Africa, International Journal of African Historical Studies,* and *The Muslim World*[2] for permission to reprint material which earlier appeared in those publications, MacMillan Publishing Co., Inc., for the quotation on page 60, and Oxford University Press for the quotation on page 50.

In 1910, E. H. Blyden wrote, in editorial correspondence to the *Sierra Leone Outlook* of the West African Conference of the United Brethren in Christ,

> A wide, a varied, a necessitous, a difficult field confronts the earnest worker in this country. The situation demands less of Europe and more of Africa; less of the letter and more of the spirit; less of theology and more of religion; less of dogma and more of Christ.

I understand the present book to be a response to the spirit of Blyden's challenge.

---

[1] See Reeck, 1971.

[2] Chapter two originally appeared in *International Journal of African Historial Studies* V, 4 (1972); chapter three in *Geneva-Africa* XI, 2 (1973); and chapter five in *The Muslim World* LXII, 3 (1972.)

CHAPTER ONE

INTRODUCTION

This is a book about the compelling moral and social bonds that tie people together in a couple of chiefdoms in Sierra Leone, and about ways in which those people have sustained and rearticulated their binding ties in interaction with Christianity and Islam during the precolonial and colonial period since 1875. The impact of modernizing influences is the theme that unites these years. The Mende people, about whom the book is largely written, refer in English to the ties that unite them by the term "deep Mende."

The geographical setting for the study consists of the Kori and the Bumpe chiefdoms of the Moyamba District of Sierra Leone. Before the imposition of formal colonial rule, these areas were designated most frequently as the Bumpe country and the Kpaa Mende country, terms both more vague and more encompassing of land area than the formal boundaries of Kori and Bumpe chiefdoms as finally fixed in the twentieth century. Kori Chiefdom centers in the town of Taiama, the traditional nineteenth century capital of the Kpaa Mende people. Bumpe country belonged traditionally to the Sherbro people, but the population contains many Mende as well as Lokko and Temne.

The traditional religions of the Mende and Sherbro are difficult to distinguish from the whole cultures of which they are part. It is sufficient to note that the traditional initiation rituals were conducted by secret societies (Poro for males, Bundu for women), that the various secret societies possessed medicines useful in manipulating universal force, and that private practitioners (*halei-mui* or "medicine men") were also held capable of manipulating force for private or social ends. Other relevant aspects of the complex religious traditions of these peoples will be introduced at appropriate points in the text.

The missionary agency of special interest is the Sierra Leone Mission of The United Methodist Church (UMC). The UMC was incorporated in the U.S. in 1968, but its antecedents with Sierra Leone missions were the Evangelical United Brethren Church (EUB, 1946-68), preceded by the Church of the United Brethren in Christ (UBC, c. 1800-1946). The first UBC missionaries arrived in Sierra Leone in 1845. The activity of this mission is of particular interest,

in part, for, unlike British mission societies in Sierra Leone, it avoided
Freetown and moved directly to the hinterland. Also, the UMC
and its antecedents were products of the American frontier revival
movements. Its missionary practices in the nineteenth century and
early twentieth century resemble closely those of evangelistic American
agencies now becoming more prominent in Africa. Thus, study of
the transformation of the UMC in interaction with rural African
societies may give insight into the possible futures of the "third
force" of American interdenominational and holiness missions to
which the attention of Africanists has recently been directed.[1]

I conceive of this study as a case study in historical sociology
with an emphasis upon religious ethics. That is, I am interested
in the development of social patterns and processes as these are
related to highly generalized symbolic commitments of actors in
situations. Following Clifford Geertz, I understand religion to be
"...a system of symbols establishing powerful, pervasive and long-
lasting moods and motivations, formulating conceptions of a general
order of existence, and clothing those conceptions with such an aura
of factuality that the moods and motivations seem uniquely realistic." [2] The studies in this volume rely heavily on social scientific
methodology, though normative judgments based on theological and
philosophical commitments are ventured in chapter six.

This book uses a comparative approach to the study of religious
ethics. Comparative religious ethics is an attempt to apply the methods
of social ethics on a crosscultural scale.[3] Until now in Western
scholarship, social ethics has focused primarily on the Western
tradition. For instance, François Houtart found it possible even
when writing on liberation movements in Southern Africa to treat
his subject with only one brief reference to the traditional socio-
cultural ethos of the African people themselves.[4] Comparative religious
ethics grows out of the Western tradition, but seeks to understand
that tradition in sympathetic comparison with other traditions. The
global situation today dictates that the study of religious ethics
should proceed in isolation no longer.

Like Christian social ethics, comparative religious ethics seeks to
be comprehensive and looks, as Walter Muelder says, for emergent

---

[1] Gray, 1968, pp. 22-23.
[2] Geertz, 1966, p. 4.
[3] Muelder, 1966, pp. 20-22.
[4] Houtart, 1972, p. 196.

coherence. Descriptive study prepares the way for normative or value-informed judgment in social ethics. In fact, it is assumed that out of the study of the how and why of human action, some notion of how men *ought* to act or to revise their action will, perhaps, emerge.[5]

I have benefitted from several past and contemporary scholars, in addition to those already cited, in my attempts to achieve some further clarity about the meaning and methodology of comparative religious ethics. Max Weber's comparative studies of religious action inspired me from the moment of first acquaintance in graduate school. Ernst Troeltsch, while benefitting from knowledge of the comparative program of sociologist Weber, went further by seeking clues to the norms of a higher, binding reality in the midst of the relativity and diversity of the given cultural traditions.[6] Troeltsch came closer than Weber to a satisfactory definition of the problem of comparative religious ethics, in my opinion.

Troeltsch began his studies from within the main assumptions of the academic movement he defined as "the modern idea of history." The modern idea of history,

> is the history of the development of peoples, spheres of culture, and cultural components. It dissolves all dogmas in the flow of events and tries sympathetically to do justice to all phenomena, first measuring them by their own criteria and then combining them into an overall picture of the continuous and mutually conditioning factors in all individual phenomena that shape the unfolding development of mankind.[7]

Troeltsch affirmed that the absolute lay beyond history, but also attested that, "the relative contains an indication of the unconditional."[8] The task, as James Gustafson indicates, then becomes "...that of finding justification for both religious belief and for moral decisions which do not deny the relativities of history, but which provide an objectivity short of absolute claims."[9]

Comparative religious ethics, in sum, involves (1) the use of social scientific concepts and methodologies, (2) in conjunction with philosophical and theological conceptions and commitments, (3) for the comparative analysis of two or more distinctive ethical or moral traditions, (4) with a view toward greater coherence, that is, a better

---

[5] Niebuhr, 1963, pp. 13-19.
[6] See Troeltsch, 1971, p. 105 and elsewhere.
[7] Troeltsch, 1971, pp. 46-47.
[8] Troeltsch, 1971, pp. 106, 115.
[9] Gustafson, 1972, p. 67.

understanding of decisions and actions persons and societies ought to take.

In its descriptive mode, ethics is the study of morality as part of the whole human context, and no account of man is precluded from providing insight.[10] Religious ethics emphasizes those aspects of the search for personal or social well being most clearly related to general symbolic orientations.

I understand the foregoing paragraphs about the nature and methodology of comparative religious ethics to be statements of general interest and direction, yet incomplete and not finalized. Considerable further theoretical work is obviously necessary before a coherent theoretical formulation of comparative religious ethics will be possible.

The social scientific aspects of this study are couched in the perspectives of modernization theory, particularly as formulated by S. N. Eisenstadt and R. N. Bellah. Following them, the modernization process is understood to be the phenomenon of a society in developing and maintaining central institutions and symbols capable of sustained growth and of appropriate responses to the continuing social, economic and political problems inherent in the process.[11] The question for this study becomes, in what ways do African traditional religion, American missionary Christianity and Maliki Islam interact with and respond to each other and to broader social changes deriving from the impact of the modernization process in rural Sierra Leone? Within the scope of this broad problem I chose to emphasize African responses particularly.

An important point to note is that the problem around which the study revolves is not so much the analysis of the modernization process itself, as such, but rather the kinds of responses emerging in rural African society to the impact of expansive cultural forces originating outside that society. One constellation of expansive forces was the association of missionary, commercial and governmental institutions of the West. Chapters Two, Three and Four emphasize the responses of African societies to these forces during successive periods in the late nineteenth and the twentieth centuries. Another expansive force impinging on rural Sierra Leone was Islam. Chapter Five is devoted especially to an analysis of the responses of Mende society to Islam.

---

[10] This definition of ethics corresponds to the conception of "Ethics Wide" given in Edel, 1968, pp. 8-9.

[11] Based on Bellah (Ed.), 1965, p. 170 and on themes in Eisenstadt, 1966.

My use of modernization theory, then, is intended as follows. (1) Modernization theory was used mainly as a systematic means of generating questions to put to the data. I trust that the patterns I identify as emergents come out of serious wrestling with the data, and not out of a facile imposition of modernization theory on the data. (2) My main interest was in the responses of rural African societies to the religious impact of expansive civilizations. The modernization process is understood as the historical context for religious interactions.

There was no particular reason in principle for choosing to study Mende, Western and Muslim interactions, nor for drawing such narrow geographical and chronological delimitations as I have done. In contrast, Joseph Smurl has recently published a comparative study of religious ethics on a global scale, and such studies as his are surely necessary for the proper development of comparative religious ethics as a discipline.[12] But I would add that I feel that research should be pursued at the micro or case study level as well as at the macro level for the full development of comparative religious ethics.

My practical reason for my choice of subject was simply that through an earlier experience in Africa in 1960-61, I became fascinated with the complexity and beauty of the African culture and wished to interact with African cultures again. Furthermore, it is one of the treasures of Sierra Leone, more precious than her diamonds and iron ore, that a rich diversity of religions is present in such small compass, and this is highly worthy of study in its own right.

Data for this study were gathered from two main types of primary sources. Archival sources were utilized to the maximum extent possible, especially the Archives of the Government of Sierra Leone in Freetown. I researched in these archives from July through early December, 1968. Archival sources were particularly significant for the study of the nineteenth century, and Chapters Two and Three rely largely on them. The approach in Chapter Two is biographical to a large extent since archival information dealt more with rural African leaders than with general data about the populace at large. The other chapters are more concerned with social institutions and processes in general.

Oral sources were also utilized to a considerable extent. The

---

12 Smurl, 1972.

gathering of data from informants consumed much of my year's time and much paper. My practice was to locate key informants from a variety of structural positions in society (e.g., missionaries, African Christians, African Muslims, Lebanese traders, old person and young persons) so as to be able to double check all data from at least two perspectives. Data gathered orally were related to archival data whenever possible, so as to afford a check from yet another perspective. It was and remains my belief that this form of research can yield valid knowledge if pursued critically. I also maintain that oral data may well yield more reliable information than library research if one's interest has to do more with cultural ethos than with theoretical or formal ethics alone. I took oral data in Kori Chiefdom from Christmas, 1968, through March, 1969, and spent April and part of May, 1969, in Bumpe Chiefdom doing the same.

I deemed it unnecessary for my purposes to conduct an independent and complete ethnological survey, for two reasons. First, Kenneth Little and other ethnographers had studied and reported extensively on Mende people (though Little investigated the Kpaa Mende to a lesser extent than the "Upper" Mende). I assumed the validity of the existing ethnographic and historical materials and built on them where possible. Second, to study religious interactions within the context of the modernization process is to restrict the nature of the problem to some extent, and therefore a complete ethnological study would have been unnecessary, even if I had been trained for and capable of undertaking it. The reader will discern that I used some methods of the anthropologist in my fieldwork, without, I hope, violence to the methods and with benefit to the study of comparative religious ethics.

CHAPTER TWO

INNOVATORS IN RELIGION AND POLITICS
1875-1896

Riverain Sierra Leone — that part of the country accessible by boat from the Atlantic coast by way of natural water routes — and its approximate hinterland supports African societies experienced in adjusting to impinging external social pressures. Historically, some of the pressures were African in origin. Others were European.

From as early as the sixteenth century, Portuguese, and later English, sought to exploit the human and natural resources of the region. However, the full force of the Western colonial surge broke over the riverain societies in southern Sierra Leone in a relatively brief period preceding and following the imposition of the Protectorate in 1896.

This chapter is intended to contribute to an understanding of ways in which African societies adjusted to the external pressures stemming from the impact of the West in the period prior to the imposition of the Protectorate. I will emphasize the responses of certain prominent rulers in the Bumpe country of Sierra Leone.[1]

Trade, politics, and missions were the three main agents of the Western impact in Bumpe country. This chapter focuses largely on politics and missions, although as commerce formed an indispensable part of the whole, there will be some mention of traders.

I will refer to the period between 1875 and 1896 as the Ante-Protectorate period. This period encompasses the time between the first decisive indications by the British of their determination to control a wide range of events in the hinterland of Sierra Leone and the formal proclamation of the Sierra Leone Protectorate in 1896. 1875 seems appropriate as a date to mark the beginning of the Ante-Protectorate period for in that year the important Treaties No. 82 and No. 83 were concluded between Governor Samuel Rowe and representatives of the Sherbro, Lokko and Mende people of Bumpe country. By the provisions of these treaties political, commer-

---

[1] The word Bumpe has been spelled variously as Bompey, Boompay, Bumpeh and otherwise, but Bumpe has gained general acceptance.

cial and even religious patterns came to be regulated to a considerable degree according to the rising demands of the Government of Sierra Leone for control over the hinterland of the colony.[2]

The boundaries of Bumpe country were defined in 1875 by the Government Interpreter, Thomas George Lawson. The boundary ran along the Ribbi (or Ribi) River and east to the Yonni and Koya (Quia) countries, then south to the Kagboro (Bago) Creek and on to Yawry Bay.[3]

Prominent physical features of the Bumpe Country include the Bumpe River, with its two major branches, and the Ribbi River, both of which empty into Yawry Bay; extensive swamps along rivers and creeks; and the relative flatness of the upland ground, broken here and there by a gently rising hill. The Banana and Plantain Islands are offshore.

The Superintendent of the Aborigines Department described the Bumpe country about 1888 from personal observation he made on trek.

> Fertile soil covered with brush wood and high grass varied by patches of parklike land. Cultivation is carried on in its primitive form by most of which is uncultivated possibly on account of the paucity of the population. Rice, cassava, Bennie seed are however grown in quantities and palm kernels and palm nuts form a no inconsiderable portion of its marketable commodities.[4] (All *sic.*)

In this chapter I intend to show that innovative, flexible patterns of rulership in the Ante-Protectorate Bumpe country can be understood in large part by historical antecedents in the dynamic African societies populating the area. In order to elaborate the nature of the inherited flexibility we turn now to a historical sketch by way of background to the Ante-Protectorate period.

I

The capacity to adjust politically and socially seems always to have characterized the peoples of the Bumpe country. The base group in the Bumpe country according to available historical sources was the Bullom Sherbro.[5] According to Walter Rodney, the Bullom

---

[2] Great Britain, Colonial Office, *Collection of Treaties with Native Chiefs, etc. on the West Coast of Africa* (London, 1892), part II, "Sierra Leone," pp. 206-09.

[3] SLA, G. I. (Lawson), "Information Relative to the Neighbouring Countries," July 24, 1875, GIM, 1873-76, p. 204.

[4] SLA, S.A.D. (Parkes) to Governor (Hay), 1889, ADLB, 1887-89, p. 342.

[5] "Sherbro" denotes the southern group of the Bullom. See McCulloch, 1964, p. 75.

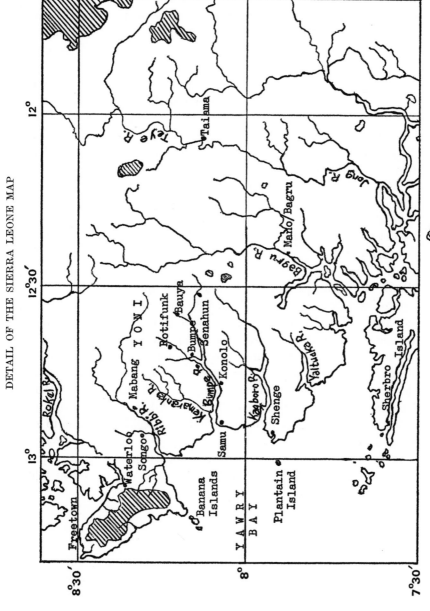

DETAIL OF THE SIERRA LEONE MAP

Elevation of 1000 ft. or more

were part of a loose multi-tribal community, the Sape, occupying much of what is now called Sierra Leone in the sixteenth and seventeenth centuries.[6] The Sape people, including the Bullom, were overrun by an invading force of people termed Mane. The Mane, though thinly spread, captured political leadership.[7]

Apparently, Sherbro kingship was a political arrangement devised in order to bind the Mane conquerors to the conquered Sherbro. M. McCulloch indicates that the first Sherbro king was said to have been named Seh Bura, from which the term "Sherbro" may have been derived.[8] Rodney states that a Mane viceroy was granted the rule of the Sherbro and that his name was Selboele.[9]

Besides Sherbro kingship, of which even the broad outlines are by no means fixed at this stage of knowledge, an institution of Sherbro queenship also existed. T. G. Lawson referred to one Sherbro queen: "Ya Comba is the Queen of the lands including lands and territories now claimed by the Caulkers..." [10] This suggests one queen ruling all the territories along the Yawry Bay. Oral evidence, however, allows the identification of three Sherbro queens ruling in these territories since at least 1800. Their locations and titles are as follows: at Shenge, Yah Kumba; at Ribbi, Yan Kai; and at Samu on the Bumpe River near its mouth, the Kong Charma.[11]

The last-named of the three, the Kong Charma, was queen of the Bendu group of Bumpe River Sherbro. Oral tradition states that the first settlers of the Bumpe country were the Bendus.[12] Later immigrant groups found it expedient to establish marriage alliances with the Kong Charma in order to obtain a legitimate right to rule as principal chiefs.

It is necessary to reconcile Sherbro kingship and queenship. A likely resolution is that the original Sherbro political system relied

---

[6] Rodney, 1967, p. 219.

[7] *Ibid.*, p. 237.

[8] McCulloch, 1964, p. 77.

[9] Rodney, 1967, p. 228.

[10] SLA, G.I. (Lawson), Memo, February 13, 1879, encl. in G.I. (Lawson) to Ag. C.S. (Crooks), February 14, 1879, GILB, 1879-81, p. 92. Fyfe, 1962b, p. 75, perhaps following Lawson, also mentions only one queen of the Sherbro.

[11] Reeck, 1971, Interview No. 134, Samu, Bumpe Chiefdom, p. 834; and No. 144, Rotifunk, Bumpe Chiefdom, p. 862.

[12] Reeck, 1971, Interview No. 134, Samu, Bumpe Chiefdom, p. 834; and No. 129, Rotifunk, Bumpe Chiefdom, p. 804.

upon rule by queens and that the Mane invasion instituted an overlord king to whom the queens related as sub-chiefs.[13]

Out of these reconstructions emerges a picture of considerably fluid social and political organization. The political flexibility of some Bumpe rulers in a later period in response to the European impact appears to have been consistent with the adaptability characteristic of the Sherbro rulers in response to pressures from African sources at an earlier period.

After the development of economic exchange with Europe, access to trading sites along the rivers of the Bumpe country became highly desired. One of the dramatic aspects of the history of the area is the in-migration of several African groups in order to establish trade contacts. A brief tracing of the developing webs of inter-relationship between the Sherbro and immigrant groups will establish a continuing proclivity to change and adaptation.

One group of immigrants into Bumpe country was the Bumpe branch of the Caulker family. I will refer to them as the Bumpe Caulkers. Together with the Shenge branch, Bumpe Caulkers have been and remain important in the modern political history of southern Sierra Leone.

The Caulker family stems from the descendants of Thomas Corker, a white trade agent in Sierra Leone for a few years following 1684, and Seniora Doll, Duchess of Sherbro and a member of the Yah Kumba family. "Their descendants, keeping the paternal surname, inherited the maternal claim to the chiefdom, which they extended to include the Plantain and Banana Islands offshore." [14] The Caulkers, controlling the slave trade on these offshore islands, grew rich and powerful.[15] The resulting ascendancy of the Caulkers led to the name "the Caulker country" for the area between the Ribbi River and the Yaltucka River.[16]

The establishment of Caulker reign at Bumpe River dates from 1820, when Thomas Caulker moved to the mainland after leasing

---

[13] Carol Hoffer suggests another resolution of the problem in a letter to me dated February 14, 1974. She states that the office of Ya Kumba can be held by either a male or female official. If her evidence is valid, the suggestion offered by Hoffer resolves the problem.

[14] Fyfe, 1962a, p. 10.

[15] Fyfe 1962b, p. 23.

[16] de Hart, 1920, p. 18.

Banana Islands to the government.[17] He signed Treaty No. 8, 1820, as one of the head chiefs in the River Cammaranca.[18] This date appears to begin the effective distinction between the Bumpe and Shenge Caulkers.

The Caulker family was notable for educational and economic archievements in the embryonic modern sector from an early date. As early as 1820, Stephen Caulker opened a Church Missionary Society (CMS) school on the Plantains.[19] It cannot be stated for certain that members of the Bumpe branch attended this school, but it is certain that many Bumpe Caulkers attended the UBC school at Shenge after its foundation in the 1860s,[20] and have availed themselves of modern education ever since.

By the 1840s the entrepreneurial endeavors of the Caulker family had shifted from slave trade to the sale of timber from the Bumpe country. Timber stands were depleted in the Rokel River and traders were turning south.[21] The Bumpe Caulkers thus, for a time, served an important function in linking European timber traders to sources in the Bumpe area.

Even while ties of these kinds were forged in the modern realm the Caulkers solidified ties with traditional institutions and symbols. An initial link was forged with the Bendus when the Kong Charma gave a daughter to Tham Bome (Thomas) Caulker.[22] Likewise two powerful Bumpe Caulker chiefs — Canraybah in the 1840s and Richard Canraybah in the 1860s — committed their loyalties to Poro.[23] Poro is the secret society for males and traditionally was extremely powerful in marshalling social control and political authority. McCulloch says it may have been supreme in the government of Sherbro chiefdoms.[24]

The Caulker family forged a new pattern of rulership in the nineteenth century by mediating between aspects of modern Western

---

[17] Fyfe, 1962a, p. 133.

[18] Great Britain, Colonial Office, 1892, p. 75.

[19] Fyfe, 1962a, p. 133.

[20] Reeck, 1971, Interview No. 115, Rotifunk, Bumpe Chiefdom, p. 743; and No. 147, Rotifunk, p. 865.

[21] Fyfe, 1956, p. 118.

[22] Reeck, 1971, Interview 134, Samu, Bumpe Chiefdom, p. 834; and No. 144, Rotifunk, Bumpe Chiefdom, p. 862.

[23] Information corresponding to Canraybah from Fyfe, 1962a, pp. 248-49. Information corresponding to Richard from Domingo, 1922, p. 7.

[24] McCulloch, 1964, pp. 81-82.

life as they began to impinge upon Bumpe country, while at the same
time welding themselves firmly to the primordial legitimating institutions and symbols of the autochthonous people.

Compared to the Caulker family, a larger immigration in terms
of absolute numbers was that of the Lokko people. The prominent
leader of the Lokko was a powerful warrior, Sorie Kessebeh, who
eventually headquartered at the town of Rotifunk. The ascertainable
facts about Sorie's life include these : (1) he came from the North;
(2) he was of the Kanu clan of the Lokko; and (3) he was called upon
by the Caulker family through Chief Canraybah to help repulse
Yonni Temne and other peoples seeking to invade Bumpe country.
In question are the date and course of his migration as well as the
precise nature of his relationship to the Caulker family.

Elizabeth Hirst, in an article on the history of the Lokko, refers
to Sorie Kessebeh (whom, using the family name, she calls Sorie
Kanu) as a leading warrior of Gowahun. He left Gowahun after a
dispute with his brother Gbanga Koba-Wa after the latter became
chief about 1840, according to Hirst.[25]

It is perhaps an error to suggest, as Hirst does, that Sorie left
Gowahun because of familial infighting. Furthermore, the factors
involved in the choice of Bumpe country by Sorie for settlement
are somewhat more complex than Hirst suggests. Reasons for these
judgments are the following. Traditional sources portray Sorie as
leaving Gowahun *in the company of his father and brothers* and settling
to the north of Bumpe country in Ribbi country.[26] From this it
appears that the Kanu migration was part of a larger movement
of Lokko people out of the Lokko heartland, spurred by Temne
pressure, not family feud.[27] According to traditional accounts, the
family later moved south into Bumpe country, settling at Konolo
to work in the timber trade. It was while he was thus occupied that
Sorie was invited by Chief Canraybah Caulker to assist in defending
the country against the Yonni and Koya Temne and the Kpaa Mende.
Hirst asserts that Canraybah needed Sorie to help oppose Madam
Yoko, but this also appears to be in error. Madam Yoko was a leader
of the Kpaa Mende, but Canraybah died in 1857 and Yoko did not

---

[25] Hirst, 1957, p. 38.
[26] The key traditional sources are Williams, 1930; and Reeck, 1971, Interview
No. 126, Rotifunk, Bumpe Chiefdom, pp. 789-92.
[27] Described in Hirst, 1957, *passim*.

become a factor in Bumpe politics until after the death of her husband Gbanyah in 1878.[28]

Upon becoming a mercenary for the Caulkers, Sorie established a series of war fences, or stockaded forts, in a line stretching from his head town of Rotifunk north and west to Gbasati near Mabang.[29] He manned this line of defense with Lokko warriors and ruled them and their families as a headman. He possessed a striking war-gown, covered with *sebbehs*, Muslim phylacteries or charms.[30] After some success in defending the chiefdom he was given permission to settle at Rotifunk permanently by Canraybah.

In the early career of Sorie Kessebeh we observe the beginnings of innovative rulership by one who lacked ties of kinship and secret society to the local populace.[31] He did not marry into the family of the Kong Charma as had the Caulkers. He gained a right to rule politically through providing a service (military defense) to the principal political authority, Chief Canraybah. These patterns intensify in Sorie's later career, as we shall see.

Elements of the Kpaa Mende people were also migrating into Bumpe country. The Kpaa Mende influenced the area increasingly during the nineteenth century. Two of their rulers, Gbanyah and Yoko, are of particular importance for the present study.

Some picture of the nature of the Kpaa Mende migration can be gained from a composite of widely confirmed traditions concerning the great leader Kori. Kori was the central figure in a party of elephant hunters who came down from Tungeah after game. They made a successful kill at a site on the Teye River. Following victory over the aboriginal Banta Temne, Kori attracted followers to his prospering settlement from Tungeah and other eastern Kpaa Mende towns. Thus was founded Taiama, the nineteenth century Kpaa Mende capital. (The Kpaa Mende were often called Taiama Mende.) Migration continued as far as Bauya and Senehun in Bumpe country. A hunter would go out, kill an elephant, put up a hut, become prominent

---

[28] The date of Gbanyah's death is found in Fyfe, 1962a, p. 418.

[29] Williams, 1930, pp. 2-3.

[30] Reeck, 1971, Interview No. 126, Rotifunk, Bumpe Chiefdom, p. 792. Cf. Williams, 1930, p. 3. It is from these *sebbehs* that the name Kessebeh was derived.

[31] There is no direct evidence that Sorie lacked Poro membership, but I think it likely because he came from the North (where Poro is weaker then in the South) and because he seems to have been firmly Muslim and, later, Christian — both of which discouraged Poro membership.

and people would go to join him. Thus were founded many villages such as Mongheri, Njama and Bauya.[32]

In 1873, Lawson wrote that Mende people settled in Bumpe country with the permission of Richard Canraybah's great-grandfather.[33] This would suggest that the Kpaa Mende migration reached the Bauya-Senehun area by as early as 1820.

Perhaps this migration was prior to and independent of any contact with the West. It is possible, however, that the Mende were trading ivory with European buyers, either directly or through intermediaries. One informant, speaking of the migration, said, "All came down in search of elephant. On account of tusks; they were selling tusks to white people." [34]

The story of early Kpaa Mende contact with the colonial powers is largely the story of the career of Gbanyah. Gbanyah was a nephew of Chief Gbenjei of Taiama. Gbenjei in turn was a son of Kori and the third successor to the Taiama chieftainship.[35] Gbanyah was thus of the founding lineage of the Kpaa Mende chiefdom centered at the capital town of Taiama.

Gbanyah appears to be an early example of those young Africans who, chafing under the necessary delays to positions of power in the gerontocratic traditional system, created innovative patterns for the achievement of political power more quickly by linking up to the Western sphere. All necessary qualifications for eventual elevation to high office in Taiama apparently were possessed by Gbanyah. But, rather than waiting until later in life for access to power and benefits of office through traditional means, Gbanyah used his skills to more immediate advantage by marketing them to Freetown's emerging demands for certain political and economic services. In the process, he, like Sorie Kessebeh, created an innovative pattern of rule.

As early as 1861, Gbanyah supplied a force of Mende warriors

---

[32] Reeck, 1971, Interview No. 46, Taiama, Kori Chiefdom, pp. 288-89; and No. 93, Mokoli, Kori Chiefdom, p. 606. Also [Kokoya-] Daugherty, 1932, p. 7; Reeck, 1971, Interview No. 67, Taiama; and Ojabemi, 1966. (In fairness to all contestants for office in Kori Chiefdom it must be noted that one Musa, said to be an elder brother of Kori, is claimed as founder of Taiama in Reeck, 1971, Interview No. 34, Taiama, p. 222.)

[33] SLA, G.I. (Lawson), Memo, September 30, 1873, in GIM, 1873-76, p. 97.

[34] Reeck, 1971, Interview No. 37, Pelawahun, Kori Chiefdom, p. 239.

[35] SLA, G.I. (Lawson), February 16, 1877, GILB, 1876-78, p. 64; also Reeck, 1971, Interview No. 41, Taiama, Kori Chiefdom, p. 257; and No. 48, Taiama, p. 312. No. 33, Taiama, appears to be in error on p. 219, where the informant is quoted as stating, "Gbenjeh [sic] had for his uncle Gbanyah."

to the British. Governor Hill had rushed troops into Koya to assist the Lokko allies of the British. Their efforts against the Temne were joined by Mende supplied by Gbanyah.[36] Many aspects of this arrangement were nothing new. Taiama Mende had been known to "sell war" to neighbouring chiefdoms for some time. Also, any alliance against the Temne, the traditional enemy, would have been welcomed in Taiama. The unique element in the incident was the mutually advantageous arrangement with a party (the government) that was interested in rationalized, centralized political control. Thus, while being rightly seen as pursuing his own ends in 1861, Gbanyah's work must also be regarded as an extension of government influence and, to that extent, cooperation in the rationalization of politics in the hinterland. Gbanyah and the government discovered a mutual interest in reciprocity.

Gbanyah was instrumental to modernization in the economic realm also. After successful destruction and looting of Temne towns he retired to Senehun on the Bumpe, where he ruled until his death.[37] Senehun became the focal point of the Taiama Mende drive toward positive contact with the West. Political and economic exchange between the Taiama Mende and the West tended to be mediated through this town. The opening of Mende-British trade at Senehun probably antedated Gbanyah's location there in 1861 or 1862. One testimony says that Gbanyah's father was the first chief of the town.[38] Trade in any considerable volume, however, developed in the 1860s. By 1862, at least a half-dozen Creole traders resided there and by 1872 Senehun boasted an entire neighborhood of Creole traders, termed by Christopher Fyfe the "British quarter." [39]

In providing for the linking of modern and traditional forces, Gbanyah may be understood as extending both Western and Kpaa Mende interests. As in the 1861 incident, Gbanyah's own point of view may well have continued as one of loyalty to the inherited Mende patterns of action. Even the recruitment of Mende warboys by him for the Ashantee Expedition of 1873 was, from his point of view, perhaps understood as "selling war" in the traditional sense

---

[36] Fyfe, 1962b, pp. 82-83.

[37] SLA, G.I. (Lawson) to Aide-de-camp (Jackson), November 22, 1881, GILB, 1879-81, p. 677.

[38] Testimony of Ebenezer Albert Lewis in Great Britain, 1899, II, p. 487.

[39] Fyfe, 1956, p. 118 and 1962a, p. 411.

and did not constitute an overweening commitment to colonial processes as he may have understood them.[40] Furthermore, Gbanyah continued to engage in the thoroughly traditional activity of plundering, indicating that his patterns of action remained at least partly traditional. But on the other hand, Gbanyah's authority and capabilities were useful to government and to traders.

Gbanyah, therefore, may be regarded as one engaged in a complementarity of functions and services that can obtain under conditions of partial engagement between modern and traditional social systems. Traditional roles may take on modern functions. The outgrowth of this coalescence of traditional and modern systems at Senehun was the drawing of the rural Bumpe and Kpaa Mende people into increasingly dense linkage with the West, its control system, and its more expansive scale in the political realm.

In summary, even before the Ante-Protectorate period one cannot fail but to note broad changes of considerable magnitude in Bumpe country. Tribal balances had shifted due to the movement of peoples in and toward the area — moving in part, at least, in response to the attraction of Western forces. The nature of change had been altered by the creation of situations in which Africans could supply economic or political goods and services desired by the West. One important result was the emergence of a new kind of ruler (e.g., the Caulkers, Sorie Kessebeh, and Gbanyah) — one who was adept in both traditional and modern spheres of activity and whose rule could be seen as a function of both African and Western interests simultaneously.

The significance of the period for the history of social change and modernization in Sierra Leone cannot be measured in my opinion by the level of modernization; for if measured by the usual indices such as new towns, political parties, and central symbols, the level was very low. The greater significance of the era for modernization is that African societies long practiced in managing internal change were proving themselves capable of responding with flexibility to the exogenous impact of the West through the emergence of rulers who could function in linking both traditional and modern social systems.

---

[40] On Gbanyah's recruitment activity see Fyfe, 1962a, p. 396, substantiated by SLA, G.I. (Lawson) to Governor (Berkeley), March 10, 1874, GIM, 1873-76, pp. 170-71.

II

After showing the nature of Western inroads into Bumpe country in the Ante-Protectorate period, I shall suggest two kinds of responses typical of African rulers of that period and illustrate by discussing the careers of two innovators in politics and religion.

Government policy during the Ante-Protectorate period was basically non-interventionist, according to J. D. Hargreaves.[41] This intended aloofness, however, became less viable as time elapsed in view of the need to protect British subjects (primarily Sierra Leonean Creoles) trading in the interior and to defend territory from the acquisitive French in the 1890s.[42]

It has already been shown that the government arranged to exercise limited control over hinterland trade, politics and religion through treaties as early as the 1870s. In 1881, the government reiterated its policy in Bumpe country : to protect British subjects; to increase trade and revenue; to suppress warfare and slavery; to allow chiefs to rule (but virtually as government agents); and to obligate British subjects to live by the laws of the countries in which they abode or traded.[43]

In Treaty No. 134 the Kpaa or Taiama Mende were brought into British jurisdiction. This treaty was concluded in 1891. The Mende chiefs promised to refer all disputes to the governor for his binding decision, to give British subjects free access to the Kpaa Mende territory for trade, to refrain from jeopardizing the lives and property of British subjects through acts of war, to refrain from making agreements with other governments and to keep up all trade roads. In consideration, the three signatories were stipended the total sum of £ 10 to be divided among the three of them (Dendeh, Degbeh and Foray Vong).[44]

Corollary to the policy on opening up the country to trade, government roads were built into Bumpe country from the colony. Roads

---

[41] Hargreaves, 1954, pp. 168-69.

[42] Information corresponding to trade from Hargreaves, 1954, p. 169. Information corresponding to French designs from Fyfe, 1962b, p. 127.

[43] This paragraph is based on the following sources. SLA, [Governor's Speech to 74 Chiefs], July 6, 1881, in GALB, 1878-82, pp. 160-61; and (Governor [Havelock]), First Draft of Agreement with Chiefs of Ribbee, Bompeh, Cockboro, and Other Districts Near Them, [1881], in Aborigines File, 1881.

[44] Great Britain, 1892, pp. 280-81.

reached Songo Town in 1862, Rotifunk and Senehun from Songo in 1878, and Taiama from Bargru in 1889.[45] The roads served as a rudimentary infrastructure for trade, as highways for show-the-flag expeditions of several governors, and as occasions for disputes between the government and chiefs over maintenance and brushing. The existence of the roads greatly facilitated the growing inter-relationship of the Western and African social systems.

Government diplomacy was operative in Bumpe country through the office of the Government Interpreter and, after 1891, the Department for Native Affairs.[46] The Government Interpreter and the Secretary of the Department for Native Affairs (S.D.N.A.) handled communications between the government and chiefs, interpreted hinterland situations, and made recommendations to the governor. Overland messengers were deployed to convey communications to and from the hinterland. Illiterate chiefs used secretaries or called upon available literate persons such as traders or missionaries when needed.[47] The records of this correspondence form a rich deposit of primary source material for the history of the area.

Gradually, the government asserted authority by taking on the function of appointing (and occasionally deposing) head chiefs in Bumpe country. This provision came into its most important use when the government exiled Richard Canraybah Caulker in 1888 for noncooperation.

The general goal of the government in all these arrangements seems to have been to encourage conditions suitable for unimpeded and increasing trade without assuming costly burdens of direct administration.

About the beginning of the 1890s the government realized that continuing unsettled conditions in the hinterland of Freetown called for a more permanent kind of influence there. The response was to station Frontier Police in key towns throughout the Bumpe and Taiama countries. "Frontiers" were stationed in Senehun as early

---

[45] Information concerning Songo from, Sierra Leone, Administrator, 1886, p. 35. Concerning Senehun and Rotifunk, SLA, Letter from Queens and Chiefs of Quiah (Bome Rufah, *et. al.*) to Governor (Rowe), April 13, 1880, GILB, 1879-81, p. 91. Concerning Taiama, Governor (Hay) to chiefs of Taiama, January 17, 1889, ADLB 1887-89, pp. 269-70.

[46] Fyfe, 1962b, p. 130.

[47] See Hargreaves, 1954, pp. 168-84. The S.D.N.A. explained his responsibilities in Great Britain, 1899, II, p. 36.

as 1882, in Rotifunk in 1889, in Quelloo (Kwellu), Moyamba, and
Taiama in 1890.[48] The size of the units varied from about five to
seven men. They reported information to the government and stopped
tribal raids.[49] These permanent constabulary forces represented a
vigorous attempt to control events in the hinterland and were indicative
of the trend toward the imposition of direct administration.

As a consequence of government action the African societies, and
in particular their rulers, were increasingly intruded upon by government force as the period progressed.

The vigor and initiative of the Sierra Leone Creole trader up and
down the West Coast has been duly noted by many a historian, and
Bumpe country experienced wide exposure to Western goods and
cultural patterns through the agency of Creoles. Both the stationary
and the itinerant traders were influential in promoting a budding
market economy and in importing Western wares such as cloth and
small household goods into Bumpe country. By the 1890s, traders
and their Westernizing influence were pervasive in the whole area,
providing means through which the masses could exchange goods
and ideas with the outside world.[50]

Traders were less explicit about their goals than either government
or missionaries, but clearly they were concerned for the exchange
of goods to their own profit. Their interests resulted in demands
upon the government for safety of person and possession, for the
collection of debts and for the recovery of stolen goods.[51] The demands
of Creoles led to pressures on rural rulers by the government for

---

[48] Concerning Rotifunk, SLA, Governor (Hay) to Inspector General of Police
(Halkett), October 19, 1887, ADLB, 1887-89, pp. 140-41. Concerning Kwellu, Governor
(Hay) to Ag. Inspector General of Police, August 28, 1890, ADLB, March-November,
1890, p. 236. Concerning Moyamba, Governor (Hay) to Ag. Inspector General of Police,
July 16, 1890, *ibid.*, p. 160. Concerning Taiama, S.D.N.A. (Parkes) to Inspector Taylor,
January 3, 1890, A/NADLB, 1890-91, p. 87. Concerning Senehun, Administrator (Hay)
to Henry T. Holland, February 26, 1887, cited in Great Britain, *Further Correspondence
Respecting Disturbances in the Native Territories Adjacent to Sierra Leone. (In Continuation
of C. 4905)*, command paper 5236 (London, 1887), pp. 66-69.

[49] Information concerning functions based on SLA, Governor (Hay) to Inspector
General of Police (Halkett), October 19, 1887, ADLB, 1887-89, pp. 140-41.

[50] On Creoles as cultural models in the hinterland see Little, 1967, p. 262 ff. Also
see Porter, 1963.

[51] When plundered, Creole traders would frequently appeal to government for
reimbursement. See, *e.g.*, SLA, The Declaration of Mary Ann Taylor before Her
Majesty's Justice, October 9, 1879, in C.S.M.P., 142/1881.

guarantees of the safety of British subjects. In these and other ways government activity interlocked with that of Creoles.

The third major aspect of the Western surge was the Christian mission activity. Although to many Western Christians the distinction between Christ and Caesar seems evident, to the Africans, missionaries often seemed to represent the same forces of imperialism as government, as truly in Bumpe country as elsewhere.[52]

The Church of God (Sierra Leonean Baptist) opened a station led by John Parker at Senehun under Gbanyah's protection in 1878; by 1884 it included schooling among its services.[53] Also, one Reverend Bowen paid a call at Taiama in 1879, but probably acted in a personal capacity rather than as a representative of his church. He was described as a Mende recaptive, ordained by the CMS. His uncle lived at Taiama.[54]

Because of its larger numbers, greater resources, and continuity, however, the Church of the United Brethren in Christ was more influential in Bumpe country than other missions. Its largest and most continuous station in Bumpe country was at Rotifunk.

The initial missionary activity of the UBC in the Bumpe country was the work of the Rev. Joseph Gomer of the Home, Frontier, and Foreign Missionary Society. He itinerated on an occasional basis in the 1870s from his home station of Shenge, and urged an expansion into the area upon the Woman's Missionary Association (WMA) of the UBC.

In 1878, the WMA established the Rotifunk station.[55] The authorizing instructions called for the opening of a school and provided for the construction of "...a substantial mud house..." for the first missionary, Miss Emily Beeken.[56]

Emily Beeken was succeeded by Dr. Mary Mair from 1879 to 1883. But the great organizational champion of the Rotifunk mission was the Rev. R. N. West, superintendent from 1882 to 1894. By 1898, with an American staff of seven and a larger African staff, the mission included a clinic, an industrial and agricultural division, a graded school, a boarding house for boys and another for girls, and a church.[57]

---

[52] Cf. Hodgkin, 1957, pp. 100-01.

[53] Concerning 1878 see Fyfe, 1962a, p. 418. Concerning 1884 see SLA, G.I. (Lawson) to J. H. Johnson, January 24, 1884, GILB, 1882-84, p. 402.

[54] SLA, G.I. (Lawson) to Aide-de-camp (Jackson), December 14, 1881, GILB, 1879-81, p. 702.

[55] Renner, 1966, p. 5.

[56] Hough, 1958, p. 18.

[57] Witt, 1898, p. 95.

Missionary policy and activity worked hand in glove with the government program in Bumpe country. Whereas in America the UBC felt constrained at times to actively work for reform in civil law, in Sierra Leone their missionaries had the deepest appreciation for the government and its traveling commissioners and Department for Native Affairs. In America, civil law and God's law sometimes appeared to the UBC to be in conflict, but in Bumpe country British rule and God's law had an apparent affinity against the backdrop of chaos and darkness perceived in the African society by the missionaries.

For instance, Dr. Mair reported with appreciation the government military action at Rotifunk to drive off invaders in 1880.[58] Dr. Mair and successive missionaries sometimes communicated local intelligence to the government.[59] In 1885, the African Committee of the WMA presented a resolution which read, "Whereas war still rages in that country near our mission, therefore, resolved, that we as an association take such steps as may be deemed advisable to secure the intervention of the government for peace.[60] The government, for its part, introduced newly-arrived missionaries to the chiefs and in 1896, through the Department of Native Affairs, strongly advised the reluctant Foray Vong, Chief of Taiama, to lease land to the UBC and permit it to work in Taiama.[61]

Though never attaining (and perhaps not desiring) the degree of temporal control and economic involvement as reported of missions in Zambia by Robert I. Rotberg, for instance, it is nevertheless apparent that the Rotifunk station exerted considerable influence among the people of Bumpe country.[62] It may be judged that among the three facets of Western activity in Bumpe country in the Ante-Protectorate period the mission was very significant by virtue of visibility and constant presence.

---

[58] EUBA, Mary Mair, "Report of the Rotifunk Mission" (unpublished manuscript presented to the Fifth Annual Meeting of the Women's Missionary Association, 1883) pp. 66-69.

[59] See, for instance, SLA, G.I. (Lawson) to the Chief of Bompeh and Ribbee (Richard Canraybah Caulker), November 23, 1882, GILB, 1882, p. 523, where he says the Governor "...was pleased to have a good report of you from Mrs. Mairs [sic]. ..."

[60] WMA, African Committee, 1885, p. 83.

[61] For an introduction see SLA, G.I. (Lawson) to Chief of Bompeh and Ribbee (Richard Canraybah Caulker), December 13, 1882, GILB, 1882-84, p. 17. Concerning Foray Vong, see S.D.N.A. (Parkes) to Chief of Taiama (Foray Vong), January 20, 1896, NADLB, 1895-96, pp. 249-50.

[62] Robert I. Rotberg, 1964.

Summarizing, during the Ante-Protectorate period three distinct but interlocking forces based in Western society — government, missions, and trade — sought to precipitate change in the African setting. "Christianity and civilization" implied a concerted and integrated attempt to foster a modern society in Western terms in Bumpe country. The one social field superimposed itself over the other. Some functional linkages between the traditional and modern systems formed, and one of the conspicuous linkages was the "new ruler."

III

Two typical response patterns to the Western impact were devised by rulers in Bumpe country: avoidance and reciprocity. Some traditional rulers (such as the Kong Charma, some of the Caulkers, the Taiama chiefs and others) sought to avoid entanglement with and resist the West. This strategy eventuated in the White Man's War of 1898. Others (whom I call "new rulers") used links with Western society to achieve desired goals of power and status.

"New rulers" refers to persons achieving positions of political power commensurate in scope (over at least several villages) and in function (judging cases, legislating and administering affairs) to that of the traditional chief but relying in part on the support of Western rather than entirely upon traditional African bases. In that such rulers devised new means of rule in the context of the Ante-Protectorate period they were distinctly innovative. (I would urge that their innovative capacity was consistent with the dynamic flexibility characteristic of pre-existing patterns of Sherbro and Mende rulers of the Bumpe area, described above.) Hence, "new rulers" are those who act out of traditional concepts of power and status but whose power rests in the function of mediating between the Western and African social fields or systems.

Since a presentation has already been made of aspects of the early career of Sorie Kessebeh in the years prior to the Ante-Protectorate period, it remains to analyze his career as a "new ruler" during the years 1875-1896. Sorie qualifies eminently as a new ruler since he managed to link the social field of Western forces with the social field of African life in a reciprocity response pattern.

Sorie skillfully achieved a measure of political security in the volatile Bumpe political life by carrying out government directives to the point where he gained government support to his claims to rule. Except for the government support it seems likely that Sorie would have had only achieved nominal jurisdiction as a Caulker sub-chief over Lokko elements in Bumpe country. With government backing he achieved much more.

The basis for the relationship between the government and Sorie was established in a meeting in December, 1881, when an agreement was reached as to proper jurisdictions in the Shenge-Bumpe area. Richard Canraybah Caulker was reaffirmed as principal chief of the Bumpe and Ribbi area. Four "principal chiefs" were appointed to be under him, including Sorie Kessebeh. The importance of this agreement for Sorie was that it gave him a status guaranteed by the government in its emerging system of Bumpe governance.[63] As a recognition of status he was stipended £ 10.[64]

After the 1881 agreement, the next factor to work in Sorie's favor politically was the heating up of the Yonni wars. The Yonni people were moving forcefully into Bumpe country throughout the earlier nineteenth century and to repulse them was Sorie's primary task under Chief Canraybah. The term "Yonni Wars", however, has come to be applied particularly to the strenuous fighting during the period between 1884 and 1887. In 1887, a British force under Sir Francis DeWinton crushed the Yonni war parties, thus ending the episode.[65]

During the Yonni wars, Sorie was the constant ally of the government in driving the Yonni from Bumpe country. In critical circumstances, inspectors were sent to Rotifunk to help Sorie prepare for defense. In 1887, the Deputy Governor wrote his thanks to Sorie for his good work in helping to settle the Yonni trouble.[66] So it is evident that his ability in warfare enabled Sorie to solidify connections with the ruling power. In this way Sori gained some independence from the Caulkers.

In 1888, almost immediately on the heels of the 1887 accolade by the governor, there followed the exile of Richard Canraybah Caulker,

---

[63] SLA, G.I. (Lawson), Memo for Queen's Advocate, October 6, 1883, GILB, 1882-84, pp. 295-96.

[64] SLA, Department for Native Affairs, "List of Chiefs in Receipt of Stipends and Annual Presents," November 6, 1896, M.P. 6501/1896, encl. in NAMP 397/1897.

[65] SLA, G.I. (Lawson), Memo, December 7, 1887, GILB, 1887-88, p. 55.

[66] SLA, Administrator (Hay) to Chief Sourie Kessebeh, April 14, 1887, ADLB, 1887-89, p. 37.

the principal chief, for implication in raids by William Caulker against Thomas Neale Caulker of Shenge in 1887. Richard was a puzzling chief. Educated in the CMS Grammar School, Freetown, one might expect him to have been more circumspect in relationship to the government.[67] He did appeal to the government for assistance from time to time, but the government came to suspect him of duplicity. Caulker's involvement in the Shenge affairs gave the government the excuse needed. Caulker was exiled to the Gambia and Gbanna (or Bannah) Will Caulker was allowed to act for him.[68] Gbanna was Muslim, illiterate in English, and a weak ruler.[69]

One consequence of the interim rule was a decrease in the power of the Caulkers over the sub-chiefs under them. The sub-chiefs came to be treated as independent principal chiefs by the government. This autonomy had been sought by Sorie, together with Madam Yoko and Canray Mahoi of Ribbi, through the cultivation of close ties with the government. (R. C. Caulker was reinstated in 1895 and immediately began to irritate the government by attempting to assert rights over Senehun and Ribbi — an indication of the measure of autonomy they in fact achieved from Caulker rule. In 1897, he was suspected of conspiracy against the Protectorate Ordinance and accused of insolence against the District Commissioner of Kwellu.[70] He was listed in the Chalmers Report of 1898 as an "ex-chief.")[71]

The government thus supported Sorie, most tangibly perhaps by the stipend but, no less importantly, morally, in return for his fulfilling certain obligations (no provocation of other chiefs nor aggressive war-making, the protection of traders, and the cleaning of the government road. Rotifunk was a principal point on the road between the Colony of Sierra Leone and up-country.) These responsibilities were spelled out by memos from Freetown

Hence, between Sorie and the government a kind of reciprocity developed in which Sorie, by tradition unqualified for the office of chief but in practice supported in office by the government, came

---

[67] See Fyfe, 1962a, p. 372, for biographical information.

[68] SLA, G.I. (Lawson) to J. C. E. Parkes, June 12, 1888, GILB, 1887-88, p. 201.

[69] For biographical information see Reeck, 1971, Interview No. 147, Rotifunk, Bumpe Chiefdom, p. 865.

[70] SLA, S.D.N.A. (Parkes) to R. Caulker, October 2, 1895, NADLB, 1895-96, pp. 123-24; and Ag. D.C. Kwalu (Barker) to C.S., May 1, 1897, encl. in NAMP, 634/1896.

[71] Great Britain, 1899, II, p. 559.

to practice the prerogatives and to enjoy the perquisites of political rule in upper Bumpe country.

It must not be thought that Sorie meekly complied with all government directives like a stooge. Actually, he maintained considerable freedom for maneuver. For instance, the Rev. and Mrs. West felt they had evidence that Sorie had surreptitiously supplied warboys to William T. Caulker in 1887 — the very sort of action for which Richard was exiled ! [72] Likewise, in one of his more doubting (perhaps more realistic) moments, Lawson penned,

> Of late Chief Sorie Kessehbeh of Rotifunk is not to be relied upon. He is more for catching slaves than to be a faithful friend to the Government and for using force to take possession of lands that are not his, which will soon bring dispute to the country.[73]

The government frequently had to warn Sorie to return plundered goods to traders or to cause roads to be cleaned. The government used the stipend like a teacher uses the recess period — withholding it to punish non-cooperation.[74] That such measures were required indicates that Sorie was his own man and managed to maintain autonomy from the government while still using the government as part of the basis of his power. Thus there was genuine give and take in the relationship between Sorie and the government.

It appears that Sorie also adroitly walked the knife-edge of reciprocity in relationship to trade and traders. This can be seen in that, on the one hand, he hosted several Creole traders in Rotifunk but that, on the other hand, he managed to permit his followers to enrich themselves from time to time by plundering traders on roads round about Rotifunk.

Sorie's relationship to the mission is of considerable interest. When the WMA decided, upon the recommendation of Gomer, to open the station in Bumpe country they seem to have chosen Bumpe Town as the site. But Rotifunk became the site. The reason for the change in venue is not spelled out in mission sources, but a local source portrays Chief R. C. Caulker as anxious to site the mission away from his capitel of Bumpe Town. He persuaded Sorie to accept

---

[72] SLA, Lida M. West to Gomer and Wilberforce, July 4, 1887, copy enclosed in unnumbered M.P. "Shaingay Raids, Unregistered Memos and Notes, 1887," in misc. file of 1887 papers.

[73] SLA, G.I. (Lawson), Memo, October 30, 1888, GILB, 1888-89, p. 32.

[74] See SLA, Administrator (Pinkett) to Chief of Rotifunk, December 18, 1884, ADLB, 1882-86, p. 196.

it at Rotifunk, even though Sorie was reluctant at first.[75] From that time on, however, Sorie gave every indication of cooperation with the mission, even converting to Christianity after some time. Some years after Sorie's death his successor came to the missionaries and, recalling how Pa Sorie and the missionaries had consulted each other about their work and troubles, said he was grieved to not enjoy the same close relationship.[76]

Sorie is quoted as having remarked, upon returning to Rotifunk from an up-country trip in 1893, that "...none of his fellow chiefs had such things as the Lord had blessed him with." [77] These "blessings" were the benefits of the mission, which included such impressive novelties as a shipment of band instruments from a church in the U.S. as well as the more substantial features — a growing mission compound with houses, chapel, school, farming, and rudimentary training in trades, and especially the missionaries themselves. The missionaries brought the prestige of the presence of white men, thus enhancing Sorie's status among his colleague chiefs, and were useful in communicating with and in influencing the government.[78]

In 1890, an upsurge of religious revivalism took place in Bumpe country during which Sorie converted to Christianity. One must remember the ecstatic intensity of the early UBC revivals. At Rotifunk in 1890 the "fire struck forth" in ways like the following. Missionaries praying all night in the chapel experienced "shocks" and "flashes." The Frontier Police, kept awake by religious conviction, developed insomnia. Rum was poured into the Bumpe by traders, while "country fashion" folk brought in medicines to be burned.[79] This atmosphere resulted in part from the prior persistent religious work of the missionaries in the compounds of Rotifunk, and partly from the visit of Amanda Smith, a black American evangelist, who spearheaded an intensive period of special revivalist preaching.[80] Sorie himself was heavily labored and finally came to the chapel, turned a somersault

---

[75] Renner, 1966, p. 5.

[76] Groenendyke, 1901. The reference is to a Yambo Sello, not the same as another successor, Santigi Bundu.

[77] Witt, 1893, p. 94.

[78] Certain of the Bantu seem to have found missionaries advantageous for similar reasons for a time. See Hutchinson, 1957, p. 161.

[79] Harford, 1934, p. 150, quoting a letter of R. N. West.

[80] Smart, 1932, p. 9.

over the altar, and confessed that God was "pulling the sin out of him." [81]

Sorie is said to have become a "real Christian," evidenced by not praying in the mosque, by renouncing polygyny, by abandoning drinking and smoking, by enacting a law against work on Sundays within his domain, and by requesting a Christian funeral (which, due to circumstances beyond his and missionary control, he did not receive). [82] The change seems great, but it had been anticipated by a long period in which Sorie's frame of reference was more and more influenced by Western forces. Further substantiation for the conversion comes from the fact that all but one of Sorie's children were Christian and several of his children were sent to schools. [83]

An observation is in order. Those most influenced in the revivals (soldiers, traders, and the chief) had already undergone a measure of social mobilization and were somewhat detached from the dominant symbols of the traditional cultural ethos. [84] The masses, so far as long-term pattern indicates, were relatively untouched.

Thus there is a positive correlation suggested between integration into the Western social structure and acceptance of Western values as transmitted through mission Christianity. In religious conversion, persons already drawn into the new framework of modernization to some extent, found a symbolic legitimation.

One need not understand Sorie's conversion merely as a case of "rice Christianity," in which converts sell their birthrights for the mess of pottage available through the mission. Sorie's conversion seems more adequately understood as a case of the development of myth in response to changing technique. [85] If Sorie's structural experiment in stitching together the two social fabrics with which he was clothed can be regarded as technique, and if myth and technique are interdependent, then his gradual assimilation of Christi-

---

[81] Groenendyke, 1921, pp. 201-02.

[82] Renner, 1966, p. 6; Groenendyke, 1921, p. 202; and Reeck, 1971, Interview No. 126, Rotifunk, Bumpe Chiefdom, p. 790.

[83] Reeck, 1971, Interview No. 126, Rotifunk, Bumpe Chiefdom, p. 790; and Renner, 1966, p. 6.

[84] "Social mobilization" is used in the sense defined by Karl Deutsch (1961, p. 494) as "...the process in which major clusters of old social, economic and psychological commitments are eroded and broken and people become available for new patterns fa socialization and behavior."

[85] "Myth" and "technique" are used in the sense of R. M. MacIver, 1965, pp. 4-5.

anity, culminating in conversion, can be seen as an experiment in a balanced response to the Western surge.

Sorie furnished an important case of a "new ruler" who found it possible to relate creatively to the impact of the West in Bumpe country while maintaining a measure of autonomy from the government by adopting the reciprocity response pattern in economics, politics, and religion.

The challenge to Sorie's experiment would have been the White Man's War in 1898. Sorie was spared this test by his death in 1897. Sorie's son and successor, Santigi Bundu, hid in the bush, and perhaps Sorie would have been forced to the same alternative to the other two choices : death along with the five missionaries of Rotifunk killed at the hands of the rebels; or connivance with the rebels in the killings.

In 1906, the government presented Madam Yoko with a medal inscribed,

Madam Yoko Paramount Ruler of the
Gpa Mendi

Chiefdom Sierra Leone Protectorate
June 1885 to August 1906.[86]

This inscription is perhaps the source of statements in M. C. F. Easmon's writing and elsewhere that oversimplify the position of Yoko in the Ante-Protectorate period and obscure the nature of her rise to power.

Much of Easmon's material is valid, especially the important paragraphs in which he describes the way in which Chief Gbanyah of Senehun acquired Yoko as wife at the funeral of Chief Gbenjei of Taiama, the husband of Yoko and uncle of Gbanyah.[87] These links to a ruling house at Taiama may have given Yoko a measure of legitimacy as a ruler; however, there seems to be no basis for thinking that she claimed descent from Kori. Therefore, she would not have been truly qualified for the office of paramount chief.

Yoko, indeed, became perhaps the most powerful of the chiefs of the protectorate during its first decade (1896-1906) when she controlled

---

[86] Quoted by Easmon, 1958, p. 165.

[87] Quoted by Easmon, 1958, pp. 166-67. Cf. Reeck, 1971, Interviews No. 41, Taiama, Kori Chiefdom, pp. 257-58; and No. 47, Taiama, pp. 298-99.

the Kpaa (or Gba) Mende Chiefdom. Her route to this pinnacle of power is dramatic.

Two stories are told of Yoko's rise to power. The first version gives Gbanyah on his deathbed asking Governor Rowe to recognize Yoko as his successor at Senehun. Rowe is reported to have acceded,[88] and thus Yoko became chief.

The second story, one of gradual growth of Yoko's power at Senehun over a period of years, appears to be the correct one. As seen above Gbanyah died in 1878. Movee was appointed chief at Senehun in Gbanyah's stead.[89] Movee was a poor chief in government eyes — a drunkard and lax on the protection of trade — and when he died in 1883 Yoko was addressed by the Governor and asked to protect the traders and their property in Senehun.[90] This probably indicates that Yoko was the effective ruler of Senehun (but not of the Kpaa Mende Chiefdom, as mistakenly stated on the medal) by that date. The choice of Yoko as chief was confirmed in 1885 when the past-due stipend was paid, on Lawson's suggestion, to Yoko. Yoko was chosen by Lawson because she had already gained a reputation for doing the "work of the country."[91] Evidently she filled the power vacuum created by the gradual weakening of Movee.

Once recognized by the government, Yoko increased her power over the people by the use of Frontier Police. When police were first requested by the war-weary Senehun traders in 1884, Yoko protested in a note to Governor Havelock that they would meddle in "country customs."[92] But Yoko soon learned to use Frontiers in order to meddle in country customs herself — to shape power relationships to her own benefit. She was resented by her own people for her crass manipulation of other chiefs by the threat or fact of government firepower.[93] In 1884, she was plundered by her own people and her neighboring Mende chiefs would not take a hand in redressing her complaints.[94]

---

[88] Easmon, 1958, p. 165, gives this version and so does Fyfe, 1962b, p. 123, though the latter compacts the first and second versions into one.

[89] SLA, Governor (Rowe) to Movee, February 23, 1881, GALB, 1878-82, p. 101.

[90] SLA, G.I. (Lawson) to Madam Yoko and Geahgbo, February 2, 1883, GLB, 1882-84, pp. 419-20.

[91] SLA, G.I. (Lawson) to Private Secretary, July 25, 1885, GILB, 1885-86, pp. 52, 53.

[92] See SLA, Havelock's reply to Yoko, May 22, 1884, ADLB, 1882-84, p. 143.

[93] Reeck, 1971, Interview No. 47, Taiama, Kori Chiefdom, pp. 298-99.

[94] SLA, G.I. (Lawson) to Private Secretary (Jackson), May 16, 1884, GILB, 1884-85, p. 98.

Yoko consolidated her grip on the Kpaa Mende in Bumpe country in 1887. Her rival for power had been Chief Commander (or Kamanda) of Bauya. Commander was a son of Gbanyah and probably had the legitimate right to succeed at Senehun in the eyes of the people.[95] Unfortunately for himself, Commander had Lawson's dislike. Lawson favored Yoko in the power struggle. In 1887, when Yonni warriors ruined Senehun, Bauya, and other lower Mende towns, Commander was accused of complicity with the Yonni and removed to the Freetown jail.[96]

In 1889, Yoko requested more constables to reinforce the Senehun garrison. In 1890 the quad numbered seven men.[97] Additional indication of her dependency upon troops is given by her pleas for reconsideration when all troops were removed in 1896 from the then-moribund Senehun in favor of more strategic locations.[98] In the 1898 White Man's War, Yoko had to flee to the British garrison at Kwellu to save her life.

Yoko was as candid as correct in a letter on the occasion of her mission to Taiama in 1893 to choose a new chief in that place. She wrote,

> They (the Taiama chiefs) again send another messenger who now told me that Chief Dendeh of Taiama is dead and they wanted me there, so I send to inform you before consented to go, as it was *through the government* I am looked upon as their leader.[99] (Italics mine.)

Yoko's power as a ruler, it appears, did not rest largely in her leadership in the Bundu society, as Easmon suggests.[100] Rather, her total subservience to British directives and her consequent ability to command superior military strength and the spending power of the stipend, which, on account of her unimpeachable loyalty to the

---

[95] SLA, Allee, *et. al.*, to Governor (Havelock), September 13, 1882, Aborigines M.P., 72/1882.

[96] SLA, Parkes to C.S., ADLB, 1889-90, p. 2.

[97] SLA, Parkes to Yoko, May 27, 1889, ADLB, 1887-89, p. 380; and Traveling Commissioner (Alldridge) to Governor (Hay), November 20, 1890, Aborigines M.P., 710/1890.

[98] See SLA, Ag. S.D.N.A. (Sanusi), minute of June 22, 1896, in NAMP 341/1896. Senehun never recovered after destruction in 1887, partly because trade shifted to the Rotifunk-Bauya road and bypassed Senehun.

[99] SLA, Yoko to S.D.N.A., July 22, 1893 in NAMP, 366/1893.

[100] Easmon, 1958, pp. 166-67.

government, was raised from £ 10 to £ 50 in 1894 upon Parkes'
recommendation,[101] account for her power.

In the political realm, then, Yoko developed a reciprocity pattern
like that of Sorie. They both accepted British direction in exchange
for British support for their rule. However, Yoko was more decidedly
dependent upon British power and thus retained less autonomy
and room for maneuver than Sorie.

Yoko's response was wholehearted in matters of trade. In 1883,
during her rise to power, Senehun was a large place with many Sierra
Leone Creole traders.[102] Yoko earned a reputation for protecting
traders and evidently became a considerable trader in her own
right.[103] Yoko followed the reciprocity response pattern in the trading
sphere.

Yoko's response to missions, however, was less positive. Despite
the prayers of many godly, Yoko was always aloof to conversion
and, on occasion, hostile to missionaries. For example, in 1884 she
lodged a complaint with the Government Interpreter against some
practices of the United Methodist Free Church mission (which had
succeeded the Church of God in Senehun.) [104]

From 1894 to 1896 the UBC pressed the Taiama chiefs to permit
the opening there of an extension of the Rotifunk mission. The
chiefs, especially Foray Vong, refused because they feared the preaching
of the mission would erode their old customs, such as Poro. The
missionaries appealed to the Governor, who responded with letters —
one in support of the mission to the chiefs and another to Yoko
requesting her to influence the chiefs to admit the mission. Yoko
vacillated and finally, reluctantly it appears, pressed the chiefs to
accede for, as she said, "As for my own part I am in readiness any
thing the Governor bids me to do." [105]

Thus in the realm of religion (as institutionalized in the mission)
it appears that Yoko was prevented from an outright avoidance

---

[101] SLA, S.D.N.A. (Parkes) to C.S., July 24, 1894; and to Yoko, September 27,
1894, NADLB, 1894-95, p. 105 and p. 162, respectively.

[102] SLA, Inspector of Police (Revington) to Inspector General (Jackson), March 17,
1883, encl. in Aborigines M.P. 35/1883.

[103] SLA, Administrator (Pinkett) to Yoko, September 15, 1884, ADLB, 1882-86,
p. 174; and Testimony of J. C. E. Parkes in G.B., Commission of Inquiry, II, p. 62.

[104] SLA, G.I. (Lawson) to Yoko, August 18, 1884, GILB, 1884-85, pp. 178-79.

[105] SLA, Madam Yoko to S.D.N.A. (Parkes), January 7, 1896, encl. in NAMP,
26/1896.

response pattern only because her reciprocity pattern in politics and trade made it impossible.

The Ante-Protectorate situation allowed persons lacking the traditional prerequisites to achieve prominence as rulers. This is one feature illustrated by Yoko's case. In functioning to link the government to the hinterland masses she got the support of government arms. The reliance upon superior force in the assertion of colonial hegemony over the hinterland is highlighted in this case.

IV

If any particular crystallization of a social structure may be regarded as a recrystallization of earlier structures of that society plus intervening pressures from outside sources, then students of change need to rely not only on structural patterns of the period they analyze but also upon antecedent historical processes for explanation.

As a case in point, innovative rulers in Bumpe country in Sierra Leone in the Ante-Protectorate period were produced by societies in which patterns and processes of rule during earlier periods had been marked by flexibility in relationships between ruler and ruled, and by ability to incorporate change. In this respect, "new rulers" were consistent with inherited patterns.

It can be shown in turn, as I will do in Chapter Four, that these "new rulers" of the Ante-Protectorate period pioneered social and political arrangements that were highly significant models for rural Africans in the Protectorate period. Therefore, it is not adequate to begin modernization studies with the beginning of the protectorate, as is ordinarily done.

The new rulers of the Ante-Protectorate period, such as Madam Yoko, learned that it is difficult to avoid linking up with one facet, such as missions, if one has already linked up with other facets of the Western surge, such as trade and politics.

Western control over African life was certainly greater in the Protectorate period than in the Ante-Protectorate period. The possibility of this intensification of colonial hegemony can no doubt be laid in part to the reciprocity response pattern pioneered by new rulers in the Ante-Protectorate period. Yet, reciprocity led to the achievement of a measure of control over colonialism by African rulers. Sorie Kessebeh proved that cooperation with the West did not preclude all autonomy but left considerable room for maneuver in various realms. Western structures and authorities did not and could not obtain total control over African action.

Finally, the study of the superimposition of the colonial social framework over the African social system of the Bumpe country allowed us to see that as the traditional and modern systems coalesced, "traditional" patterns of action took on "modern" functions. Some roles of new rulers could be understood as rooted in the histories of social innovation in their respective cultures. On the other hand, the same roles could be understood as functions of colonial interests. In such cases, a distinction between the inner meaning and the outer, objective structure of the new role might be of value, but even so, the seeming clarity of the difference between traditional and modern seems to become irretrievably blurred.

What remains clear? At least the capability of African societies of the Bumpe and Kpaa Mende countries to adapt flexibly from within their own frames of reference to the rationalized and technologized forces of the Western impact. In particular, "new rulers" arose to link the West and African society, and, among them, Gbanyah and Sorie Kessebeh especially were able to obtain some social benefits from the government, traders and missionaries through a reciprocal process of give and take.

CHAPTER THREE

PROTEST AND CONFLICT, 1896-1898

The Sierra Leone Hut Tax War of 1898, seen from the perspective of the British, was one of that irksome kind of colonial war necessarily waged about the turn of the century in various locales throughout the empire. From the perspective of African societies in the Sierra Leone Protectorate, the war was novel in that virtually all of the tribal groups in the protectorate rose up in one accord against a common enemy — the colonial intruder.

The war had two theaters. The Temne or northern side has been analyzed and interpreted by La Ray Denzer and Michael Crowder.[1] The Mende or southern side has been less thoroughly explored, although Little includes an account in his book.[2] This chapter deals with the Mende side of the war in the Bumpe and Kpaa Mende countries only, and not with the entire southern theater.

Hereafter, I will generally use the Mende term *puugwei* ("White Man's War) rather than Hut Tax War, because the Mende terminology reflects the African conviction that the cause of the battle was broader than the issue of the Hut Tax alone. The Mende terminology also places the burden of proof on the colonialists, where it rightly seems to belong. The *puugwei* should be understood as a defensive, not a rebellious, action.

As we have seen, by the 1890s, the three-pronged modernization process had become institutionalized in the Bumpe and Kpaa Mende countries. These regions had become tied to the central colonial government through treaty arrangements and stipendiary relationships. The central government was represented in these regions by detachments of police. Creole traders were moving up from the riverheads further into the interior to offer modern goods in exchange for produce. Communications were being sped along government roads. Formal education had begun to spread under missionary auspices, and some rural Africans were joining with Europeans and Creoles in mission congregations in three or four villages.

---

[1] Denzer and Crowder, 1970; and Denzer, 1968.

[2] Little, 1967, pp. 43-59.

Cooperation with government, traders and missionaries had already proven rewarding to certain aspirants for power in the African societies. Through a reciprocal relationship with Western forces, some Africans advanced faster and further in society than would have been possible otherwise. Such persons we called "new rulers" in the previous chapter, and the biographies of Sorie Kessebeh of Rotifunk and Madam Yoko of Senehun were presented as particular cases in point.

On the other hand, the government pacification program had threatened the traditional prerogatives of some Africans, particularly war leaders and secret society heads. As a result of these tendencies, a cleavage was emerging between the reciprocity pattern of the new rulers and the avoidance pattern of the others.

In this chapter, I will argue that the provisions of the Protectorate Proclamation of 1896 and its subsequent implementation altered relationships between modernizing forces, new rulers and traditional rulers by radically highlighting the conflicts between Western and African social styles. The consequences included a drastic opening of the cleavage between the Africans in power, the alienation of the bulk of rural society from the West and, finally, the *puugwei*.

I

The last two decades of the nineteenth century witnessed a rapid evolution of government objectives for the hinterland of Sierra Leone. In the 1880s, government goals were limited to the promotion of a stable and safe framework for trade. During the 1880s, however, traders and trade associations campaigned with determination to get the government to assert more active control over rural areas. For instance, in 1884-85 at a mass meeting in Freetown, a resolution was framed and handed to the government calling for the following steps in the hinterland :

(1) peace should be maintained by force of arms;
(2) steps should be taken to stop intertribal slave trade;
(3) adequate protection should be given to traders;
(4) high roads leading to the interior should be protected by troops and police.[3]

In addition to having to make a response to the trading community, the government under Frederic Cardew (he became governor beginning

---

[3] S.D.N.A. (Parkes), Appendix J, May 31, 1898, Great Britain, 1899, II, p. 143.

in 1894) began to assume a moral burden for the enlightenment of the peoples of the hinterland. As Cardew put in (in retrospect),

> The Government is under a moral obligation to civilize, educate and raise to a higher standard of life these natives of the Protectorate, and this can best be done by facilitating communications by means of railways and roads, encouraging missionary enterprise by substantial grants-in-aid, not only for the education of the natives in the three R's but for giving them industrial and technical training, and by opening up the country to trade. ...[4]

In addition to its assumed moral obligation and to the demands of the trading community, the government was also anxious to preserve its sphere of influence, and thus its markets, from encroachments by the French. Thus, after negotiations, an agreement between Great Britain and France was signed at Paris on January 21, 1895, fixing the boundary between Sierra Leone and French possessions to the north and east.[5]

The result of these pressures was a series of proposals by which the government was to impose control over the hinterland. Governors Rowe and Fleming, in the early 1890s, put forward schemes for hinterland administrations. After tours in the hinterland in 1894, 1895 and 1896, Cardew put forward a scheme which varied but little from earlier ones.[6] The Protectorate of Sierra Leone was formally established by proclamation on August 31, 1896. It is important to emphasize that the protectorate was simply imposed, without any particular regard for the will, nor solicitation of the assent, of rural people or their leaders.

What was the nature of the protectorate as it was communicated to rural tribal leaders? An archival source shows that chiefs received the following interpretation in a written communication from the Secretary for Native Affairs. First, the governor, subject to approval of the Secretary of State, could depose any chief who was judged unfit for his position and appoint a successor. Second, a system of three courts — the Chiefs' Court, the Court of the District Commissioner and Chiefs and the Court of the District Commissioner alone — was

---

[4] Great Britain, 1899, I, p. 133.

[5] Appendix II, Item I in *ibid.*, II, pp. 553-54. Cardew told hinterland chiefs that if England were to not throw protection over them, the French or the Liberians or some other power would occupy the territory and perhaps not deal so considerably with the chiefs as the English did. See the "Text of an Address Given by the Governor to Certain Chiefs of the Karene District at Freetown, 15 Nov. 1897," in *ibid.*, p. 585.

[6] S.D.N.A. (Parkes) in Great Britain, 1899, II, p. 143.

to be instituted. Besides a graduation of offenses from lesser to greater import through the three courts, the District Commissioner's Court was to handle all cases between "country" people and British subjects. Furthermore, all grants of land made by "country" men to any persons not "country" men must be approved by the governor. The Queen took to herself rights to mine for gold, precious stones and minerals. Finally, slavery was proclaimed illegal. All persons brought within the protectorate to be sold or placed in servitude or pledged for debt were free. Persons presently enslaved could redeem themselves for not more than £ 4 for adults and £ 2 for children.[7]

Furthermore, chiefs were informed that their authority

> ...is now maintained and supported, not by war, raidings, and brute force, at the cost of lives of liberty of their people, but by the power of the Government. ... I want all Chiefs to understand that the Government wishes to rule the country through them, and that it is therefore to their interest to support the Government.[8]

In addition to the Protectorate Proclamation, an additional ordinance was passed in 1897 that bears on the argument. In 1896, Be Sherbro of Yonni led a group to Freetown to protest the Protectorate Ordinance. Unsatisfied by the government response, he returned home and got the Poro society to embargo the sale of produce to Creoles and Europeans in his locale. Government reaction was to pass the Poro Ordinance, prohibiting the use of Poro or any similar organization to restrain trade.[9]

The government intended to administer the protectorate with a skeleton crew so as to keep administrative expenses low. The entire area was divided for administrative purposes into five districts, and each was to be provided with a resident District Commissioner, equipped with a small staff.[10] It was assumed that little supervision would be necessary for loyal chiefs who stayed within the Protectorate Ordinance. Such chiefs would be backed politically by the government and would be given advice about ways of realizing value from produce such as rubber, gum, cotton and so on.[11]

---

[7] SLA, Ag. S.D.N.A. (Sanusi) to Chiefs in the Protectorate, October 21, 1896, NADLB, 1896-98, pp. 134-36.

[8] "Text of an Address Given by the Governor to Certain Chiefs of the Karene District at Freetown, 15 Nov., 1897," Appendix II, Item XXIII, Great Britain, 1899, II, p. 584.

[9] Fyfe, 1962a, pp. 556-57.

[10] *Ibid.*, pp. 542-43.

[11] SLA, True copy of Circular Letter No. 1 from D.C. Ronietta (Hudson) to Chiefs, July 22, 1897, encl. in NAMP 313/1897.

In addition to the protectorate administration itself, detachments of Frontier Police were to be stationed in each district to keep order. In 1896, the expenses of the Frontier Police came to £ 19, 927, an amount more than one-fifth of the total revenue of the colony.[12]

In order to pay for the costs of the administration of the protectorate and of the Frontier Police, Cardew proposed a House Tax of 5/- per house per year and 10/- a year for houses with more than four rooms. The House Tax came to be called the Hut Tax in common usage. The tax collection was made the responsibility of the chiefs.[13] As Cardew explained the matter to the chiefs.

> The cost of the administration of the Protectorate and of the Police Force, which is required to maintain peace and order therein is, in round numbers, £ 30,000. Now it is impossible that the Revenue of the Colony can meet this amount, and the Government therefore has decided that the inhabitants of the Protectorate must contribute towards the expense, especially as they are directly benefited by the Government that has been set up.[14]

One of Cardew's favorite projects for hinterland development was a railroad. He recommended, as a result of knowledge gained on his tours, that the route run through Songo Town, Rotifunk and Bo, and on toward the frontier at a line roughly parallel to the coast, cutting across the Bumpe and Kpaa Mende countries. [15] The trade generated by the railroad would bolster government revenues through taxes and tariffs.

UBC missionaries stationed in the Bumpe and Kpaa Mende countries appreciated government plans for progress in the protectorate, and saw themselves as participants in the unfolding of civilization there. For example, in 1898, the Taiama missionary L. A. McGrew wrote, "Civilization is coming, and may the Lord help us to get this people ready for it. What is done must be done *quickly*." [16] At the same time, Cardew looked with warm approval on the school education and industrial training being offered by the Rotifunk mission.[17] In fact, of missionaries in general, he said,

---

[12] Fyfe, 1962a, p. 543.

[13] Fyfe, 1962a, p. 543.

[14] "Text of an Address Given by the Governor to Certain Chiefs of the Karene District at Freetown, 15 Nov., 1897," Appendix II, Item XXIII, Great Britain, 1899, p. 584.

[15] Fyfe, 1962a, pp. 529-30.

[16] McGrew, 1898, p. 103.

[17] Great Britain, 1899, I, p. 128.

> I have always found missionaries to be the very best pioneers of civilization in
> every sense of the word, and they have always given their ready cooperation in
> the civilizing endeavors of the District Commissioners.[18]

In 1898, he recommended the disbursement of a small treasury
balance in the form of grants to the mission schools in the protectorate.[19] Thus, the program of the mission was clearly seen by the
government as part of the general colonial endeavor, and the mission
tacitly agreed.

As noted above, the government thought in terms of a moral
mandate for colonialism. A typical governmental statement of the
moral justification of the protectorate is contained in the following
quotation from a writing by the Traveling Commissioner T. J. Alldridge :

> The Protectorate Ordinance... brought about great reforms in the removal of
> oppression; the administration of justice to the Hinterland folk and the abolition
> of slavery; and also gave great confidence to the people to work and develop
> the resources of their country. Naturally, by its introduction of moral principles,
> and the breaking up of many native customs repugnant to civilized ideas, it was
> distasteful to certain persons who had profited by the old state of things. To the
> masses of the people, however, that Protectorate Ordinance must have come
> as a release from the many forms of tyranny that had been their inheritance from
> time immemorial.[20]

Moral considerations aside, the net effect of government endeavors,
with missionary and commercial support, was the creation of an
institutional framework designed to induce social mobilization and
modernization.[21] The protectorate was a new political unit much
larger in territorial scope than any of the antecedent chiefdoms,
and consisted of rationalized, centralized legal and administrative
agencies. It offered legal and physical protection for modern economic
activities, and made provision for the increase of formal education
in technical and agricultural spheres. It radically heightened the
impact of the West on the rural societies.

---

[18] *Ibid.*, p. 128.

[19] SLA, Governor (Cardew) to C.S., January 3, 1989, in NAMP 8/1898.

[20] Alldridge, 1901, p. 392.

[21] See Kilson, 1966, pp. 14-15, where he also interprets the protectorate as a means
toward more extensive and intensive modernization.

II

After the promulgation of the provisions of the protectorate, the government immediately began to receive protests and complaints from rural tribal leaders. Selected examples of such complaints are presented below, chosen especially for their relevance to the Bumpe and Taiama areas.

As early as November, 1896, the month after the proclamation of the protectorate, Madam Yoko addressed the S.D.N.A. stating her willingness to give the new ordinance a trial and her confidence that the government would amend any provisions found to be too difficult. She made no specific complaints at this time.[22]

But in late 1896, the governor, who went about the protectorate to explain the ordinance, held a meeting at Shenge at which R. C. Caulker and elders from the Bumpe country were present. At least one woman at that meeting urged Chief T. N. Caulker (of Shenge) to refuse to accept the ordinance and the Hut Tax, but he did not speak up because he feared to contradict the governor.[23] In October, 1896, the chiefs of Bumpe-Mende (near Bo) petitioned the governor to the effect that they would not pay the tax.[24] In January, 1897, rumors began to reach Shenge that interior Mende countries including Taiama would bring war upon any who paid the tax.[25]

In addition to such verbal complaints, rumors and petitions, other factors indicated growing hostility toward the protectorate. In October, 1897, the Frontier Police at Rotifunk seized forty kegs of gunpowder judged by the Acting District Commissioner to be intended for use in resisting the payment of the tax.[26] An itinerant trader reported that he could obtain no housing in Rotifunk in November, 1897, because the people were retaliating against the government-imposed tax.[27] Fourteen of nineteen roads patrolled in Ronietta District in

---

[22] SLA, Madam Yoko to S.D.N.A. (Parkes), November 3, 1896, enclosure in NAMP 574/1896.

[23] Testimony of George Maximilian Domingo in Great Britain, 1899, II, pp. 475-76.

[24] Great Britain, 1899, I, p. 19.

[25] Testimony of George Maximilian Domingo, Great Britain, 1899, II, p. 476.

[26] Information corresponding to seizure in SLA, Ag. D.C., Ronietta (Hood) to S.D.N.A. (Parkes), October 26, 1897, enclosure in NAMP 355/1897; and corresponding to D.C.'s judgment, Ag. D.C. to C.S., March 15, 1898, *ibid.*

[27] Testimony of Frederick W. Dove, trader, Great Britain, 1899, II, p. 79.

October, 1897, were rated as bad, indicating a flagging sense of duty toward the government by the chiefs.[28]

The further reactions of Madam Yoko, Chief of Senehun in Bumpe Country, are worth thorough study, since of all the affected chiefs, none was more cooperative with the government. In October, 1897, she indicated that her subjects were making three kinds of complaints about protectorate rules. First, slaves were getting their freedom; second, women were deserting their husbands, saying that the government did not allow persons to make claim of other people; and third, individuals disguised as policemen were taking wives from chiefs and others by force.[29]

When time for chiefs to collect and pay the Hut Tax drew near, Madam Yoko accepted her responsibility, but said she would fail if she were not given the assistance of government officials because (1) people did not agree to pay, (2) people were threatening her because she was acting with the government in the matter, and (3) the sight of government officials would arouse dread in the people and they would have to pay. In November, Parkes assured her of the protection of the government.[30] The correspondence highlights Madam Yoko's growing dependence on the government in the light of the situation brought about by the protectorate. Madam Yoko, loyal to government, stood increasingly in polarity against a nearly unified opposition of other chiefs and commoners. The force of the protectorate was to clear out the middle ground and intensify the cleavage in rural society.

In the face of continuing signs of growing resistance, the government continued to work toward tax collection, increasingly falling back upon the threat of force and the use of force.

In Ronietta in October, 1897, the D.C. reminded his chiefs by circular letter that they must pay the tax on the first of January, 1898.[31]

---

[28] SLA, Officer Commanding Frontier Police, Kwalu (Johnson) to Ag. D.C. Kwalu (Hood), October 30, 1897, enclosure in NAMP 354/1897. (Chiefs were held responsible to clean government roads in their districts.)

[29] SLA, Madam Yoko to [Ag. D.C. Ronietta (Hood)], October 26, 1897, enclosure in NAMP 357/1897.

[30] Madam Yoko to S.D.N.A. (Parkes), November 10, 1897, NAMP 375/1897, quoted in Great Britain, 1899, II, p. 591. Parkes' reply: SLA, S.D.N.A. to Madam Yoko, November 6, 1897, Confidential Aborigines/Native Affairs Letter Book, 1889-98, pp. 137-38.

[31] SLA, True copy of circular letter No. 2 of D.C., Ronietta (Hudson) to Chiefs, October 1, 1897, enclosure in NAMP 313/1897.

Shortly afterwards, he sent a second letter conveying a reply from the Secretary of State to an antiprotectorate petition from northern chiefs. He ended his letter with a tacit acknowledgment of the existence of resistance in his district :

> I trust that the reply of the Right Honourable the Secretary of State for the Colonies will remove any misapprehensions which you may have had with respect to the Protectorate Ordinance.[32]

Shortly thereafter, with the D.C. on leave and with signs of resistance still growing, Cardew replaced the Acting D.C., a physician, with an officer of the Frontier Police, S. Moore. The actions of Dr. Hood, Moore and the police of Kwellu are detailed in Fyfe's accounts, and included seizures of the property of chiefs, exchanges of gunfire, violence toward the persons of chiefs and a mass jailing of Ronietta chiefs at Kwellu.[33] In January, 1898, the governor directed D.C.s to disarm any armed groups in Ronietta and other districts.[34] Moore himself testified that he knew he had been sent to Ronietta because the tax would have to be collected by force.[35]

Among others, Foray Vong of Kpaa Mende country was a victim of governmental force. In 1897, he reported that he had not received his stipend since 1893, and in turn he was reimbursed the four stipends due him.[36] Perhaps on account of the receipt of the stipends, Foray wrote a warm letter to the governor in December, expressing good feeling toward both the governor and the new UBC mission in Taiama.[37] But in January or February, rumors circulated to the effect that Foray was resisting the Hut Tax.[38] A prisoner at Kwellu stated that Foray had been brought to the prison and made to promise to pay the tax. When he consented, he was let go.[39] But then the Acting D.C. went to Taiama, seized Foray's goods and brought them to Kwellu. At some point in this sequence the chief

---

[32] SLA, True copy of circular letter No. 3 of D.C., Ronietta to Chiefs, October 1897, enclosure in NAMP 316/1897.

[33] Fyfe, 1962a, pp. 558-59.

[34] SLA, Governor (Cardew) to C.S., January 15, 1898, NAMP 56/1898.

[35] Testimony of Samuel Moore, Great Britain, 1899, II, p. 467.

[36] SLA, D.C. (Hudson) to S.D.N.A. (Parkes), September 25, 1897, enclosure in NAMP 312/1897.

[37] SLA, Chief of Taiama (Foray Vong) to Governor (Cardew), December 2, 1897, enclosure in NAMP 397/1897.

[38] Testimony of George Maximilian Domingo, Great Britain, 1899, II, p. 477.

[39] Testimony of Pa Nembana in *ibid.*, p. 124.

appeared in Freetown with a large retinue to lodge his personal complaint against this treatment.[40]

Richard Canraybah Caulker also felt the sting of government power. In February, 1898, he asked for police to assist him in collecting the tax.[41] His request was refused, and instead he was threatened with arrest.[42] When he did not pay, a patrol was sent under Captain Warren to Bumpe country. Encountering resistance, the government men destroyed several towns and then discovered that the chief had fled.[43]

Overall, some tax was collected, but the collection depended on the use of force. Before the war broke out, a total of about £ 2,500 was evidently taken from Ronietta District.[44] By the end of April, 1898, the government was moving to reinforce its detachments in the area. Even so, only about forty men were stationed at Kwellu; others were scattered in detachments about the district, including one group of about four at Rotifunk.[45]

In sum, during the period of early opposition in 1897 and 1898, the hitherto slowly growing duality in African society was suddenly heightened and thrown into sharp relief as opposition to colonial government took definite shape. Some chiefs who had waivered prior to the proclamation of the protectorate moved over to the side of the resistance. The few Mende and Sherbro chiefs still allied with the government came to depend more than ever upon the backing of central power, which furnished needed defense against their own people.[46]

After over a year of warning, the Hut Tax War finally erupted in February, 1898, under the leadership of Bai Bureh in the North of Sierra Leone.[47] The northern wing of the war continued through

---

[40] SLA, S.D.N.A. (Parkes) to C.S., February 1, 1898, NADLB, 1896-98, p. 327.

[41] SLA, Chief of Bompeh (Caulker) to S.D.N.A. (Parkes), February 9, 1898, encl. in NAMP 76/1898.

[42] SLA, Minute by Governor (Cardew), February 8, 1898 in NAMP 76/1898.

[43] SLA, D.C. Ronietta (Fairtlough) to S.D.N.A. (Parkes), April 1, 1898, NAMP 73/1898.

[44] Testimony of S. Hood, Great Britain, 1899, II, p. 5.

[45] SLA, Affidavit of Harold Galway Warren, November 20, 1911, encl. in Governor (Merewether) to L. V. Harcourt, GCDSS 94/1911. (Cited after this as Affidavit of Warren, GCDSS 94/1911.)

[46] Particularly Madam Yoko, Madam Nancy Tucker of Bargru and Neale Caulker of Shenge. See Great Britain, 1899, I, p. 44.

[47] Denzer and Crowder, 1970, pp. 169-70.

1898, physically separate from the Mende wing. Psychologically, however, the successes of Bai Bureh probably emboldened the Mende for their own *puugwei*, which broke out on April 26.[48] Special Commissioner Sir David Chalmer's brief summary sketches the general framework of the southern war, helpful for understanding the clashes in Rotifunk and Taiama in particular :

> Within less than a week the male British subjects in Bandajuma, Kwallu and Sulymah Districts, with few exceptions, were murdered. A number of women also were murdered, and after an order went forth from the leaders staying the killing of women, they were treated as captive slaves. All property belonging to British subjects were plundered, except at Bonthe and York Island, which were saved by the arrival of the Marines and troops.[49]

The establishment of the mission at Taiama in 1896 was discussed earlier.[50] During 1897, an African mission worker, I. A. Inskip, opened a small school and completed a mission house.[51] In November, 1897, he was joined by an American couple, the Rev. and Mrs. L. A. McGrew, and a woman physician, Dr. Marietta Hatfield. Dr. Hatfield soon returned to Rotifunk for the reason of ill health.[52] During this period (1897-98), Taiama was an observation post for the Frontier Police, but they were withdrawn in March, 1898.[53]

On April 29, 1898, the Frontier Police post at Kwellu was attacked, and the inspector in charge decided that it was impossible to reach Taiama in order to protect the missionaries.[54] Hence, from April 29 on, Mende forces effectively isolated Taiama from government protection. On May 1, Kwellu was attacked again by a very large force said to have originated in Bandajuma and to have been joined along the way by many persons.[55] While Kwellu was under siege, the Rev. and Mrs. McGrew were held captive in Taiama for several days. At one point, it is thought, they could have escaped by hammock, but they were detained by the illness of their servant.[56] A large

---

[48] Great Britain, 1899, I, p. 47.

[49] *Ibid.*, p. 46.

[50] See p. 32.

[51] Witt, 1897.

[52] Witt, 1898, p. 95.

[53] SLA, Affidavit of Warren, p. 3, GCDSS 94/1911.

[54] *Ibid.*, p. 4.

[55] Testimony of S. Hood, Great Britain, 1899, II, p. 6.

[56] Renner, 1966, p. 7, in agreement with SLA, Affidavit of Warren, p. 2, GCDSS 94/1911.

attack on Kwellu failed on May 7. Some warboys are thought to have gone to Foray Vong in Taiama and to have stated that they would never successfully achieve victory at Kwellu so long as the McGrews were held alive. They demanded and received permission to kill the missionaries, and did kill them on May 9.[57]

Evidence at the trials of the persons charged with the murders indicates that Foray Vong assured the McGrews of his ability and willingness to protect them during the days preceding May 9, but that he finally acceded to pressure from the warboys and gave the missionaries up to be killed.[58]

At the time of the *puugwei*, Rotifunk was an observation station with a detachment of three frontier police. In addition to the six missionaries, they formed the bulk of the "stranger" population, though some Creole traders also lived there. The regular population of the town consisted of Lokko and Temne, estimated at about 3,000.[59]

The Chief of Rotifunk then was Santigi Bundu, the son of Sorie Kessebeh, lately deceased.[60] Santigi Bundu's English name was David Livingstone Kessebeh II, which he may have adopted during his school days at Shenge or in the Church Missionary Society Grammar School at Freetown.[61]

A trader who lived at Masanki in Ribbi country remembered Sierra Leoneans fleeing from Rotifunk to Freetown as early as April 19 with the message that war was coming.[62] On Sunday, May 1, Creoles from all over the vicinity poured through Rotifunk, fleeing for Freetown. The missionaries, remembering the Yonni Wars and other raids, were generally somewhat diffident to rumors of war. But as

---

[57] The date is given by Renner, 1966, p. 7. Information corresponding to warboy demands is given in SLA, Affidavit of E. C. D.'H. Fairtlough, November 24, 1911, enclosure in GCDSS 94/1911.

[58] SLA, *Regina v. Gpawa, Fassineh, Koniwah*, December 14, 1898, certified true extract from a record book in custody of Chief Justice of the Supreme Court of Sierra Leone, December 19, 1911, by Attorney General (Wilbraham), enclosure in GCDSS 94/1911. (Cited after this as *Regina v. Gpawa*.) Oral evidence is consonant. See Reeck, 1971, Interview No. 39, Taiama, Kori Chiefdom, p. 248 and No. 47, Taiama, pp. 295-97.

[59] SLA, Affidavit of Warren, p. 5, GCDSS 94/1911.

[60] Testimony of J. C. E. Parkes, Great Britain, 1899, II, p. 60.

[61] Reeck, 1971, Interview No. 126, Rotifunk, Bumpe Chiefdom, April 23, 1969, p. 789, indicates that Bundu's school was Shenge. Williams, 1930, p. 1, says that his school was the Grammar School. Whether he attended one or both, Santigi Bundu was no doubt identified with "civilization" because of his education, and thus became a target of the rebels.

[62] Testimony of Teslime Williams, Great Britain, 1899, II, p. 404.

the serious nature of this war threat became apparent, they sent the boarding pupils to their homes. In the evening, the booming of guns in the Kwellu attack was heard in Rotifunk.[63] On May 2, the news came that a trader, Mr. Coker, had been caught and killed while attempting to make his escape down the Bumpe River by boat.[64] That route of escape was thus seen to be closed. In the evening the three policemen, inadequately supplied to fight a prolonged conflict, fled.[65] Chief Santigi Bundu also fled the town at about the same time.[66] By this time the town was full of Mende warboys from upcountry, and Lokko warboys from Rotifunk and surrounding villages joined them.[67] On May 3, the faithful mission worker, Thomas Hallowell, disguised in war dress, helped the missionaries attempt an escape by foot. The missionaries, however, were captured and killed. Those killed were Rev. I. N. Cain, Mrs. I. N. Cain, Ella Schenck, Mary C. Archer, M.D., and Marietta Hatfield, M.D. These five plus the McGrews made a total of seven, and together they are referred to as the missionary martyrs. (An eighth was in Freetown on a shopping trip when the war broke and thus escaped death.) [68]

In Rotifunk, everything was destroyed : the war fence, the houses, and the mission.[69] Creole traders were killed and their shops plundered both at Bumpe Town and at Rotifunk.[70]

Forward construction on the Sierra Leone Railway was halted when workmen on the line between Waterloo and Songo ran away from their jobs on May 4, 1898, due to fright of war. The existence of the line in operation as far as Waterloo probably saved that town from destruction. Troop trains were dispatched from Freetown to protect Waterloo.[71]

---

[63] Renner, 1966, p. 7.

[64] *Ibid.*

[65] *Ibid.* and Affidavit of Warren, pp. 5-6, GCDSS, 94/1911.

[66] SLA, Affidavit of Thomas F. Hallowell, January 19, 1912, enclosure in GCDSS 16/1912.

[67] SLA, Affidavit of Peter Wyndham, November 24, 1911, enclosure in GCDSS 94/1911.

[68] Memorial tablet, Martyrs' Memorial Church, Rotifunk. The missionary on the shopping trip was Arthur Ward. Cf. Hallowell, 1928, p. 18.

[69] Reeck, 1971, Interview No. 108, Rotifunk, Bumpe Chiefdom, April 10, 1969, p. 700.

[70] There is much evidence of destruction. See, e.g., SLA, Statement of Frederick Taylor, July 11, 1898, enclosure in NAMP 224/1898; and S.D.N.A. (Parkes), minute of July 7, 1898 to C.S. in NAMP 264/1898.

[71] See Testimony of John Scobie, Great Britain, 1899, II, p. 534; and Best, 1949, p. 16.

Material damage at the river towns of Bumpe and Palli was light and the chapels in the latter towns were unmolested.[72]

Parenthetically, fighting during the *puugwei* caused some disruptions in African internal affairs. During the breakdown of central political control, some old intertribal boundary disputes were revived, intergroup fighting erupted and some Mende villages near Taiama were destroyed.[73] Besides, a couple of informants indicated that the whole populations of one or two villages around Taiama simply walked upcountry as far as Bo, returning home after the fighting. To aid in more thorough understanding of the war, these aspects ought to be pursued by ethnohistorians.

The government soon rallied, and sent two expeditions overland into Mende country to crush the Mende. The first left Freetown on May 9, under Colonel Woodgate, and the second left on May 31, under Colonel Cunningham.[74] Perhaps even before May 9, Hallowell, who had escaped from Rotifunk to Freetown, guided troops from the H.M.S. Fox, regrouped into three lighter vessels, up the Bumpe River to Yenkissa and Senehun.[75]

The Woodgate column, marching to relieve Kwellu, reached Rotifunk on May 15. Chief Santigi Bundu accompanied the column and tried to induce the townspeople not to oppose the military operations. The townsfolk did not offer active opposition, but they did temporarily abandon the town.[76] It was probably at this time that officers buried the bones of the missionaries.[77]

During the uprising, Madam Yoko and two other progovernment Kpaa Mende chiefs, Kokoya and M'biriwa, had taken refuge at

---

[72] SLA, Thomas E. Smart to S.D.N.A. (Parkes), May 16, 1898, NAMP 172/1898. For information corresponding to chapels in Bumpe and Palli, see UBC, 1899, p. 5.

[73] Information concerning burnings by Temne of Waiima town in Reeck, 1971, Interview No. 55, Waiima, p. 341; of Mokundi in Interview No. 62, Mokundi, p. 378; of Vaama in Interview No. 72, Vaama, p. 468; of Fogbo in Interview No. 76, Fogbo, p. 522; and of Njolohun in Interview No. 96, Njolohun, p. 648. All in Kori Chiefdom.

[74] Great Britain, 1899, I, p. 51.

[75] Hallowell, 1928, p. 22. Elsewhere, Hallowell names the "Countess of Derby" not the "Fox." See SLA, Hallowell to S.D.N.A. (Parkes), May 19, 1898, enclosure in NAMP 177/1898.

[76] "Report of Field Operations from Sierra Leone between 9th and 31st May, 1898," Great Britain, 1899, II, pp. 633-34.

[77] Renner, 1966, p. 7.

Kwellu.[78] After joining D.C. Fairtlough's force of police at Kwellu, Woodgate's column moved against Taiama on May 24, and oral evidence indicates that M'biriwa guided the troops.[79] (M'biriwa, Kokoya and Santigi Bundu, along with Yoko, played the reciprocity role to the end.) Taiama's great complex of fortified villages, once estimated to have housed about 10,000 inhabitants, was destroyed.[80]

The Cunningham column attacked the Mende in the Southeast, touching at Bonthe, Mafwe and Bandajuma.[81]

The government charged several persons with the murders of the missionaries. Four persons, including Chief Foray Vong, were convicted for the murders at Taiama, and three more for the murders at Rotifunk.[82] Santigi Bundu, for some reason, was tried for the murder of the Rotifunk missionaries also, but was acquitted. The case for the prosecution broke down only after, it is said, Chief Smart and George Keister (a former mission boy) suborned some of the prosecution witnesses. Later Santigi Bundu was convicted of plundering the mission house and was sentenced to fourteen years imprisonment.[83] One wonders if justice were done in this case, because, as we have seen, other documents indicate that Santigi Bundu was as endangered during the uprising as the missionaries themselves.

---

[78] SLA, Affidavit of I. A. Inskip, December 18, 1911, enclosure in GCDSS 94/1911.

[79] Information concerning Woodgate's column from Testimony of E. C. D.'H. Fairtlough, Great Britain, 1899, II, pp. 284-85. Concerning M'biriwa see Reeck, 1971, Interview No. 33, Taiama, Kori Chiefdom, p. 216; and No. 37, Pelawahun, Kori Chiefdom, January 11, 1969, p. 240. M'biriwa was an important farmer, not a warrior, before 1898. He was of the ruling house descending from Kori through Gbenjei. M'biriwa was the son of Gbenjei and a son-in-law of Yoko since Yoko had been a wife of Gbenjei before his death. Upon Gbenjei's death Yoko was given to Gbanyah. See Interview No. 33, Taiama, pp. 214-17.

[80] "Report of Field Operations from Sierra Leone between 9th and 31st May 1898," Great Britain, 1899, II, p. 634. Also, J. R. King, 1899, p. 94.

[81] "Report, 31st July 1898, Lt.-Col. Cunningham, Commanding Mendi Expedition : Operations in Mendi Country," Great Britain, 1899, II, pp. 635-40.

[82] For information corresponding to Foray's conviction see SLA, *Regina v. Foray Vong*, September 24, 1898, certified true extract from a record book in custody of Chief Justice of the Supreme Court, December 19, 1911, by Attorney General (Wilbraham), enclosure in GCDSS 94/1911. The other Taiama convictions are recorded in *Regina v. Gpawa*. For information corresponding to Rotifunk convictions, see *Regina v. Morgbeh, Bayou and Sango Woro*, September 27, 1898, enclosure in GCDSS 94/1911.

[83] SLA, Affidavit of E. C. D.'H. Fairtlough, November 24, 1911, enclosure in GCDSS 94/1911.

III

An explanation of the causes of the Hut Tax War was furnished recently by Denzer and Crowder. They summarized their understanding in the following way.

> The reasons the Temne, and later the Mende, decided on rebellion were complex. Those over and above the hut tax and the desire for independence fall under four main headings : (1) loss of authority and prestige by the chiefs, in particular their loss of judicial authority; (2) interference with traditional custom; (3) resentment at the abolition of the slave trade and the liberty offered to domestic slaves by the British; and (4) hatred of Frontier Police.[84]

This is a valid and useful statement based on an inductive study of the Hut Tax War itself. In the following section the *puugwei* will be interpreted in a different way, using the concepts of modernization theory to set some facets of the event into a more comprehensive framework of understanding. The line of argument will be that the implementation of the Protectorate Proclamation so radically escalated the claims of government to control African affairs that virtually all Africans except the "new rulers" and other moblized Africans became alienated from the government and all its Western allies. The bulk of hinterland society was virtually forced over to the side of traditional symbols and warfare in order to reassert any measure of autonomy at all.

The dramatic events of the *puugwei* brought to sharp focus the matter of the real conflict in style between a threatened African society and its self-appointed tutors, the Western forces of government, trade and missions. The term "social style" is used here to denote not only characteristic behavioral patterns of a society, such as the institutional arrangements for social control, but also the basic common assumptions that underlie the institutions.[85]

In modernization theory, the contrast between the two social styles of these two general types has often been summarized by speaking of traditional versus modern values. I would like, in a few paragraphs, to briefly enumerate in a more detailed fashion some of the specific identifiable contradictions between the styles in question — those of the West compared to those of the African rural societies.

The conflict in the social realm is most usefully understood as the contradiction between an ascriptive and an achievement society.

---

[84] Denzer and Crowder, 1970, p. 178.
[85] Cf. Redfield, 1968, p. 61.

In an ascriptive society, social status is allocated by virtue of accidents of birth, such as sex or social position of one's parents. In an achievement society, social status is allocated by virtue of the accomplishments of the individual within the accepted guidelines for legitimate competition. The contrast between achievement and ascription is never absolute; all societies depend on both modes of status allocation to some extent. The point I wish to stress is that the emphasis in Mende society was toward ascription, and in the Western society toward achievement, to such a degree that a real conflict ensured.

When the implications of the Protectorate Proclamation became clear, it was evident that accustomed methods of status allocation among African societies were precluded in some instances. This disruption affected such generally acknowledged ascriptive relationships as the subordination of slaves to masters and women to husbands. One may legitimately doubt that the British, even in their noblest dreams of moral mandate, sought to intervene in any dramatic and immediate sense in customary patterns of family life. Yet, in the short years between 1896 and 1898, wives and slaves, in positions traditionally understood as subordinate, saw in colonial control a pretense for disregarding the claims made by husbands and masters on their persons. The consequence, probably unintended by the British and certainly undesirable to husbands and masters, was insubordination. The exact magnitude of the insubordination is indeterminable, but from the evidence cited earlier the degree of social disruption seemed highly significant to rural African leaders.

In the realm of political organization, the Protectorate Proclamation envisioned a change in the type of relationship obtaining between ruler and ruled. In the Mende or Sherbro chiefdoms, relationships between rulers and the ruled were mediated by personal ties such as kinship, common membership in secret societies and direct access from family head to village head to section head to paramount chief. The protectorate envisioned the imposition of a new sort of relationship to a distant queen, a remote governor and district commissioners that one must ultimately obey though one might never personally know or even see. Though not as readily apparent as the conflict between achievement and ascription, the difference between personal and impersonal ruler-subject relationships was as pervasive and significant in its long-term implications.

Paralleling the move to depersonalize political ties, of course, was the assimilation of the relatively small and local chiefdom units

into a centralized national, even imperial, political framework. To
the British authorities in the 1890s, it seemed perfectly proper that
the global extension of British civilization in the form of the empire
should be realized through a great hegemony built of the many native
tribes and empires from the Canadian West through Africa and India.
But to the ruling families of the Bumpe and Kori countries, it must
have seemed a gross infringement on local sovereignty to be forced
to take account of the directives of a distant governor in so many
details of daily political affairs. Structurally, the chiefs were sandwiched
into the administrative scheme of the protectorate as subordinates
in a position for which there was no apparent legitimation in either
the old ways or, as yet, the new. The changes in political structure
imposed by the protectorate led to a conflict of interest between
the government and chiefs embedded in traditional understandings
of the office, and no doubt this conflict became quite impressive
to chiefs who, like Foray Vong of Taiama, were imprisoned or forced
to march to Freetown on occasion to seek redress.

In the economic realm, the most general form of conflict arose
between the commercial capitalism of the West and the subsistence
patterns of the hinterland. Capital wealth, in the form of many
dependents and certain forms of material property, existed in Mende
society, and mechanisms existed for the acquisition and allocation
of such wealth. But, in general, it seems safe to assert that Mende
and Sherbro people generally sought to maintain or preserve their
level of wealth by reference to past levels. Individual chiefs certainly
sought to accumulate increases of wealth over time, but the village
masses continued from year to year at a subsistence level, while the
capitalization of Mende society as a whole probably tended to remain
about constant over time.

Western capitalization took material and monetarized forms and
was rationally pursued with a view toward ever larger increases.
These differences between Western and African economic processes
led to specific conflicts between colonialism and important segments
of African society. It is in this context that the Hut Tax and the conflict between Mende warriors and Creole traders can best be understood.

The Creole traders, marching up with their wares from the riverheads into the Bumpe and Kori countries, were the leading probes
of the Western market economy. They were followed by the road
and bridge builders, by Frontier Police, and finally by the early
phases of the construction of the railroad. These groups and facilities

were functions of capitalism, and thus devoted in principle to profitable enterprise.

Over against the Creole traders and the supporting colonial infra-structure stood the Mende warriors. One traditional method of redistribution of wealth in Mende society was raiding. Warriors defended the wealth of chiefs and chiefdoms from raids, and made raids when appropriate to capture wealth. When Creole traders appeared on the scene, they were fat plums for the picking to the warriors, even if, in some cases, the Creoles were under the protection of a particular chief. But the continual raiding of Creole traders was in principle intolerable to the Freetown government, because capitalism seeks as great a measure of control over the variables in the economic environment as possible in order to ensure the orderly process of exchange. At first, as we have seen, Freetown tried to control raiding by diplomacy and Frontier Police. Later, the protec-torate was instituted, in large part to protect trade, and the Hut Tax was proposed as a method of financial underwriting for the administration.

The point to be emphasized here is that a significant conflict crystallized in the years 1896 to 1898 between the African and Western styles of economic organization. The conflict focused most apparently around the Hut Tax and the Creole/warboy disputes, but actually involved basic differences in orientation about both the means and the ends of the economic organization of society.

The final basic conflict between the African and Western styles centered around the Mende propensity to safeguard their cultural uniqueness versus the Western propensity to universalize their culture. The Mende seemed to wish to preserve what they were as a people. They turned inward and enshrined the full meaning of Mende culture in the secret lore of the Poro. The colonialists, however, under the universalistic implications of Christian monotheism carried along on the high tide of the expansive Victorian industrial civilization, sought to convert and to assimilate all particular cultures into a universal culture. This is the significance of the "moral burden" expressed by various government officials and missionaries. The conflict arose because the leaders of Mende/Sherbro society had an equally serious burden to protect the full meaning of their societies both from general exposure and from cultural extinction.

Again in this case, the conflict between African and Western styles was not absolute. African society had already shown itself flexible and able to accommodate certain features of Western society. That some accommodation could, in principle, be made to Western ways was not the question, therefore. The real question was about the basis for accomodation, and whether that basis would mean a radical denial of the meaning of Mende existence as understood by Mende.

The church, through the agency of UBC missionaries, stood on the side of the West in all the political, social and economic conflicts mentioned above. The missionaries supported the government and traders both morally and practically, and were committed in practice to the global spread of Western culture. But the critical role of the missionaries in precipitating the *puugwei* related mostly to the question of the universalization of culture and the denial of Mende forms of self-understanding.

It is probable that the government and traders would have tolerated secret societies so long as the latter did not unduly interfere with the harvesting of produce and with trade. This would have led to a compromise whereby the final meaning of Mende life would have been indefinitely extended through time. But to the missionaries, the claims of the secret society contravened the claims of the one God. Also, the secrecy was too much like that of Masonic orders in America, which had historically been opposed by the UBC. Furthermore, the various ritual spirits and figures of the secret society seemed fearful and devilish. In short, the UBC missionaries radically opposed secret societies and thus were no doubt perceived as hostile to the very central commitments of Mende culture and traditional religion.

In summary, the Protectorate Proclamation of 1896 and its implementation immediately thereafter radically heightened conflicts between African and Western society. This is not to say that African and Western societies were completely dissimilar. They had much in common, as is recognized elsewhere in this paper. But it did become apparent during 1896 to 1898 that many chiefs, masters, warriors and household heads had much to lose in the arrangements envisioned in the protectorate, and in fact the foundations of African society themselves were perhaps imperiled by Christianity as understood by the UBC missionaries of that era.

The main force of the Protectorate Proclamation was a clearing of the middle ground of African society. Those "new rulers," school-boys, government employees and traders already dependent on Western forces became even more wholly dependent on the colonial government, and at the same time more alienated from African society. The rest of African society coalesced at the opposite pole around traditional offices and symbols, and girded to fight.

The implementation of the protectorate and the ensuing *puugwei* brought to surface some contradictions within rural Mende society. Even though these contradictions were not of the magnitude of the contradictions between the colonialists and the African societies, they did bring about a division in tribal leadership that was important for the way in which reconstruction proceeded after the defeat of the African defenders.

In the chronological review of the *puugwei* it was shown that the Poro and warrior elite groups remained structurally independent of the newly formed colonial framework, whereas civil chiefs were divided between cooperation with and opposition to the government. These patterns of response were characterized as "avoidance" and "reciprocity."

Among the major chiefs in the Bumpe-Kpaa Mende countries, the provisions caused most of them, including Richard Canraybah Caulker and Foray Vong, to adopt unequivocal resistance to British power. Others, especially Madam Yoko, became more dependent on the colonial government than ever before. Hence, a structural cleavage among the elite gradually occurred during the late 1890s.

It was rational for chiefs to cooperate with the government as long as cooperation enabled them to achieve symbols of status readily transferable to the traditional status system. But by stating its intention to free slaves, to stop wars and in permitting Frontier Police to exercise jurisdiction over chiefs, the government undercut the basis for this reciprocity pattern by reducing the status of chiefs. The resistance of men such as Canraybah and Foray Vong can be accounted for by this blockage of the avenues of status achievement.

The progovernment elite stands out in relief. Consisting of chiefs largely dependent on government support and their relatives (Yoko and her son-in-law M'biriwa; Santigi Bundu; and the Smarts of Mahera); Creoles; mission workers; and school children (the last-named constituted a potential emerging elite), the socially-mobilized element found itself alienated from the bulk of hinterland society for the time being. Yoko's own sub-chiefs, for example, charged her with bringing the government to the country and of being the cause of their loss of slaves as of selling the country for money. Against such charges and threats that went with them, Yoko could only rely on government to a greater degree.

As a result of the situation brought about by the protectorate, therefore, Mende society developed a distinct cleavage; and at the same time, the relative size of the elite identifying itself with modernizing forces was diminished by defections.

If the Mende *puugwei* could be put down so quickly by government troops, how is it that the defenses of colonial society were so weak as to be completely swept aside by the Mende attack when it occurred? When the *puugwei* was organized, all groups identified in any way with the government were dependent upon military defense provided by the government. All other means, such as persuasion, police action, diplomacy and other forms of political control, were rendered ineffective by the militancy of the *puugwei*. Unfortunately for its dependents, the government under-estimated the potential strength of its opposition, and therefore failed to arm itself properly for defensive action. But why was defensive action needed at all? Why was the protectorate so universally rejected?

Several important factors leading to the African rejection of the protectorate have already been cited. One more factor is that mass consensus or moral legitimation for the new colonial society was lacking among rural folk, and the government seemed unaware of this fact. The supporting symbols or common values necessary to legitimate political centralization were lacking.

The mission to some extent attempted to symbolically justify the protectorate and the Hut Tax to the people. For example, a Shenge missionary, L. Burtner, preaching from Luke 20:25, asserted that the tax was justly instituted, that the people should pay and give to the government what belonged to the government while giving to God what belonged to God.[86] The content of sermons preached at Rotifunk is unknown, but at Bumpe and Palli a Creole UBC agent, Joseph B. W. Johnson, advised that God said that people must pay the tax. At the same time, Johnson discredited traditional symbols in his itinerations by burning worship sites, or in his words, "devil-houses," in villages about the Bumpe country.[87]

Despite such attempts to formulate binding symbolic ties, the actual accomplishments in this regard were no doubt minimal outside the few groups already relatively advanced in mobilization. No mutually acknowledged value center united the forces of the West

---

[86] Testimony of Alphonso T. Caulker in Great Britain, 1899, II, p. 292.
[87] Johnson in Great Britain, 1899, II, pp. 462, 464.

with the traditional societies in the hinterland. The modernizing symbols and institutions became more exposed and vulnerable and ultimately broke down completely, if only temporarily, as hostility against the protectorate increased.

The antithesis is that the traditional frameworks were reenforced and the traditional symbolic values became temporarily dominant throughout the Bumpe and Kpaa Mende countries. For instance, the great uniting sign of the Mende rebellion was the half-burned palm leaf. The war message was conveyed by runners carrying palm leaves, and raiding parties carried this sign on expedition. The half-burned palm leaf is the symbol of the Poro society, and thus stands at the symbolic heart of traditional society.[88] There are also strong indications that both general strategy and coordination of the Mende attacks were devised in and carried out by Poro.[89]

At the height of the *puugwei* the forces of modernization were at their weakest, and the ties binding the Bumpe and Kpaa Mende peoples to Freetown were at their most tenuous state. The breakdown of modernization was severe.

The forceful reimposition of government control precipitated a significant alteration of the social status system and legitimate rule in rural Sierra Leone. As the superiority of British military strength began to impress itself upon them, many chiefs faced the facts and submitted to the government. For example, the chiefs of Ribbi country tendered their submission at Songo Town, but were directed to submit to the D.C. at Kwellu, who informed them of the terms of surrender.[90] Chiefs who remained loyal to the government throughout the *puugwei* expressed fear of returning to their homes, but were assured that they would be provided with sufficient government protection.[91] Madam Yoko was awarded a silver medal for loyalty, symbolically expressing her superior position in the new scheme of things.[92] Missions were invited to join with government in continuing the civilizing mission, especially through the teaching of productive

---

[88] Great Britain, I, p. 46.

[89] *Ibid.*

[90] SLA, Governor (Cardew) to S.D.N.A. (Parkes), June 13, 1898, NAMP 222/1898.

[91] Santigi Bundu and M'biriwa returned to their towns with the troops. Thomas Smart of Koya was assured that his family had the protection of the police at Mabile. For information on Smart, see SLA, minute of the S.D.N.A. (Parkes), November 16, 1898 in NAMP 259/1898.

[92] SLA, S.D.N.A. (Parkes) to C.S., September 17, 1898, NADLB 1898-99, p. 154.

arts of agriculture and handicraft.[93] The WMA decided at its convention in 1898 to reopen work as soon as possible.[94] The central-peripheral framework of Freetown and the hinterland was reestablished.

One key difference between the situation before the *puugwei* and the situation afterwards was, as Cardew correctly observed, that the country had been conquered with the force of arms.[95] This leads me to believe that the most significant conclusion to be drawn in regard to the whole incident of the *puugwei* in respect of African responses to the West was that the conquest by force in itself brought about for the first time the formation of precontractual symbols necessary to justify colonial rule. Little says that the only precedent known to the Mende by which one people could claim right to dominate and regulate the affairs of another is military conquest.[96]

The emphatic feature is the role of force in maintaining and justifying the modernizing process in this case of colonialism, as in so many other places. Force, not persuasion or political coercion, effectively established the social authority of the allied agencies of modernization. Modernization of the Bumpe and Kpaa Mende countries was less a case of spontaneous emergence, and more a case of necessary adjustment to radical changes once rejected and then reimposed from the outside.

The timing of the Protectorate Administration was, of course, a critical factor. The radical nature of the provisions of the protectorate was partly a function of the haste with which they were imposed. Had the Europeans been content to bide time, to build ties on a basis of respect and trust to expand the basis for reciprocity and to act like guests instead of masters, the process of impact and response would surely have been different. But the Victorians were in a hurry to leave their mark on history.

In sum, the government, supported by commerce and missions, sought to hasten the modernization process through the imposition of the Sierra Leone Protectorate. The secret societies, warriors and most civil chiefs responded with an organized and vigorous military defense of their sovereignty, but were defeated by the superior

---

[93] See Chalmer's remarks in Great Britain, 1899, I, p. 84.
[94] Witt, 1898, p. 96.
[95] Great Britain, 1899, I, p. 103.
[96] Little, 1967, p. 56.

weaponry of the British troops when the government organized to retaliate.

The problem presented to African society in view of the defeat was to devise means of responding with integrity to the impact of the West within the narrowly delimited options open to a defeated people.

CHAPTER FOUR

TRANSFORMATIONS OF MISSIONARY CHRISTIANITY IN THE TWENTIETH CENTURY

*In all great reversals of human relations or attitudes
the old, superseded by the new, still lives
recessively and awaits the chance
of dominance.[1]*

In this chapter, the continuing responses of African societies to the ongoing process of modernization will be traced through the period of reconstruction following the Hut Tax War of 1896.

The modernization process went through two major periods from 1875 to 1898. The first period witnessed the gradual quickening of Western trade, governmental and missionary activity in the Bumpe and Kpaa Mende countries. While some African rulers avoided contact, others developed a relationship of reciprocal exchanges of services and status with the West. The second period, 1896 to 1898, witnessed an attempt to radically quicken modernization through the imposition of the protectorate, leading to a violent defensive war staged by African forces against the West, and the triumph of the British over the African forces.

The protectorate continued after the Hut Tax War much as it had been envisioned earlier. A key difference in the postwar setting was that the inevitability and legitimacy of British rule was established by virtue of the triumph of their military victory.

Since it was proven unfeasible to push the Western forces back to the Sierra Leone Peninsula and hold them there, African society had to devise another form of response to modernization. The thesis of this chapter is that the strength and adaptive capacity of major strata in the African society enabled them to find ways of engaging and "traditionalizing" patterns introduced by the West. Our focus will be primarily on educational, technical and cultural patterns introduced by missionaries, seen within the broader social context of the modernization process in general.

---

[1] MacIver, 1965, p. 208.

As indicated in Chapter One, the UBC mission maintained a large station at Rotifunk in Bumpe country from 1875 and an extension at Taiama, principal town of the Kpaa Mende, from 1896. The missionaries met with a degree of success in recruiting Africans — notably persons already socially mobilized to some extent — into ecclesiastical and educational institutions.

I

Political power relationships between the government on the one hand and African rulers and societies on the other were radically altered by the defeat of the African forces of protest in the Hut Tax War. In the nineteenth century most African chiefs considered themselves to be autonomous political agents dealing on equal terms with the Queen of England. By virtue of British military victory in 1898, however, chiefs had no choice but to assume the role of local administration in addition to their traditional responsibilities. Centralized authority and effective means of control characterized colonial rule of the hinterland. Together, colonial government and chiefs, to the extent that the latter cooperated with central government, were agencies of modernization in the hinterland.[2]

Stimulation of agricultural production and commercial activity in the hinterland were dominant government policies. The rail line was pushed through the Bumpe-Kpaa Mende areas by 1902.[3] Improved footpaths ("hammock roads") were constructed to traverse Kori and Bumpe chiefdoms in the 1910s and 1920s. Money order service came to Rotifunk in 1902, and patrons from Taiama could travel fifteen miles to Mano over a hammock road, and after 1926 over a motor road, for money orders.[4]

These developments enabled private firms and Lebanese merchants to move into the chiefdoms in order to exploit commercial possibilities. Taiama became a bulking and distribution center by about 1910, and Rotifunk developed into the major point for the transfer of fish from river transport to rail for shipment up and down the line. Thus Kori and Bumpe chiefdoms had access to new imported goods and

---

[2] See Kilson, 1966, and Riddell, 1970, pp. 48-55.

[3] Best, 1949, p. 22.

[4] SLA, Colonial Postmaster General to Colonial Secretary, *Report for 1908*, May 31, 1909, encl. in Governor (Probyn), Despatch 334/1909 to Secretary of State (Crewe).

to markets for cash crops, and occupations in trade and administration were open to those who qualified.

Social change paralleled economic and political change. Out of traditional rural society a modernizing sector, with supervisory, professional, and laboring categories, slowly emerged in the twentieth century. Expatriates and Creoles figured prominently in the upper strata of the modernizing sector in the first five decades of the century but were rapidly being replaced by educated protectorate folk in the sixth decade and even earlier in both chiefdoms.

II

Against the background of social mobilization in the late nineteenth and early twentieth centuries we turn now to an analysis of missionary goals for institutional Christianity and methods devised by them to implant this import into hinterland soil.

Missionaries did not consider it their fundamental purpose to modernize. Two missionaries who served in Taiama from 1925 to 1950 stated as their primary purpose in Sierra Leone:

> Wife   : Our main purpose in going... was to give Christ to the people.
> Husband : Yes. I was an evangelistic missionary.[5]

On the basis of such data and inferences from behavior it is my impression that the conscious, overt goals of missionaries were to convert, to build up a self-supporting church, and to serve in humanitarian ways to demonstrate their understanding of divine love. The missionaries of the UMC stressed spiritual conversion and disciplined church life, primary and secondary education, practical or "industrial" education and scientific medicine. They wished to mobilize Africans, to be sure, but only within the ecclesiastical structures they hoped to build.

For purposes of analysis I will propose two major thematic components of the model of institutional missionary Christianity and indicate the mechanisms developed for implementation of each component.

The first was the universalization of Christianity within Kori and Bumpe chiefdoms. That is, missionaries wished to achieve universal adherence to Christianity.

---

[5] Reeck, 1971, Interview No. 6, Indianapolis, Ind., p. 31.

The major vehicle designed to achieve this was the itineration method of village evangelism, which was used successfully and extensively in Kori but not in Bumpe chiefdom, in the twentieth century. The system amounted to a coordinated plan whereby missionaries and employees of the mission walked out over the bush paths and hammock roads from Taiama to its subsidiary villages to preach there on a regular basis. In 1917, when the Taiama station was under the supervision of the veteran Minnie Eaton, 297 itinerating services were held in villages around Taiama. C. W. Leader, Miss Eaton's successor, employed special peripatetic evangelists, teachers in the mission school and scholars to itinerate. In 1926, only one year after his arrival, Leader was able to report that on a particular Sunday 33 boys itinerated in 26 villages, preaching to 1,332 persons.[6]

An ordained African, B. A. Carew, was pastor of the Taiama Church from 1937 until the middle 1960s. Carew had been raised in the chiefdom, served as Leader's houseboy and obtained secondary and college education in Freetown. As Leader was also stationed at Taiama until 1950, Carew's practices closely followed Leader's in the matter of itineration, though Carew effectively refined the system. A visiting U.S. bishop wrote the following description of Carew's itinerating operations :

> After considerable failure five years ago, this pastor went to his knees, and God revealed through prayer the method he was to follow : that he should go to these villages and seek converts who would witness to their people and invite them to the church services and to the pastor's home for instruction and counsel.
>
> Each Sunday, following the services, an average of about fifty of these villagers come to the pastor's home. The Lord blesses the simple meal of rice and stew which Pastor and Mrs. Carew provide, and then some hours are spent in explaining the new birth and Christian way of life which demands forsaking of jujus, idols, and giving up all but one wife. After about two years of such instruction, the converts are ready for baptism and church membership.[7]

Other vehicles such as language work and recruitment of hospital patients to conversion were also used, but above all it was the intensive and extensive itineration that led to the development of village Christianity in Kori chiefdom.

The second major component in the missionary model of institutional Christianity was the regularization of the behavior of converts. This

---

[6] EUBA, C. W. Leader to General Secretary (Ziegler), Taiama, July 25, 1926, in Board of Missions Correspondence, 1926 folder.

[7] Warner, 1954, p. 9.

can be subdivided into disciplined churchmanship and Westernization.

The strict discipline expected of converts by the missionaries was largely due to the pietistic tradition of the UBC. To give evidence of a changed life was to contribute time and talent to the church and to refrain from wordly behavior. Specifically, polygyny, ancestor worship, secret societies, drinking of alcoholic beverages, smoking of tobacco and promiscuity were on the forbidden list (although some of these came to be winked at in practice after a time). A high rate of participation in church affairs was expected and, in theory if not in practice, clear boundaries demarcated the church from surrounding society.

A second aspect of the regularization of the lives of converts was Westernization. Although as seen already missionaries thought of themselves not as "Westernizers" but as evangelists, Westernization was implied in their understanding of evangelism because the UBC form of Christianity was closely identified with rural American social patterns. The following cultural standards were communicated to converts as desirable : the use of the English language including literacy, formal education, Western dress and names, monogamy, companionate marriage, scientific medicine and public health measures. In addition, an ethic of hard work and personal discipline was constantly enjoined. The "old boys" of the Taiama mission school vividly remember Leader's example of vigorous physical exertion on the farm, in the woodworking department and in building construction.

The vehicles developed in Kori and Bumpe chiefdoms by the mission to institutionalize these goals were the primary school, especially the boarding and industrial departments, the health centers and health education.

A notable feature of the missionary model of Christianity is that it embraced an inherent dilemma between commitment to both strict religious standardization and universalization.[8] One can readily appreciate that a desire for greater progress toward universalization would suggest relaxation of rigid standards in order to decrease resistance to conversion. Because of the inherent tension, members of African society could select elements that seemed appropriate as judged from the context of their respective value systems, and

---

[8] Yinger, 1970, p. 234 discusses the dilemma of religious leaders as a source of religious differentiation.

thus adopt only selected aspects of missionary Christianity. This possibility was enhanced by the fact that missionary Christianity never became the "official" model of religion in the African society but had to compete in a pluralistic setting with Islam and the various social and private traditional African religious practices.

III

Insight into the process of the transformation of missionary Christianity cannot proceed without some further understanding of Mende-Sherbro frames of reference. It appears that the greater differences in African frames of reference in Kori and Bumpe chiefdoms were not tribal (Sherbro/Mende) nor those stemming from inter-chiefdom rivalry, but structural (townspeople-villagers).[9] Hence the following analysis applies to two strata common to Sherbro and Mende people of both Kori and Bumpe chiefdoms.

Some commitments were traditionally shared by Mende and Sherbro of both the town and the village. The salient ones seem to be pragmatism in religion and secrecy.[10] Unlike Europeans, who seem to wish to universalize their styles of life, Kpaa Mende and Sherbro guard the deep core of their cultural values within the veil of secret societies. No Mende could compromise the secrets of a secret society and still be counted a full Mende.

Town Mende, however, enjoyed a social dominance over village Mende, and can thus be regarded as a traditional elite. It appears that responses to the impact of the West in the early twentieth century were determined in part by whether one was more closely allied to the decision-making town stratum or to the subordinate and obedient village stratum. (While making this broad distinction for analytical purposes, it is recognized that in practice there were gradations in both town and village strata in the precolonial period, as well as later.)

The traditional ruling town elite were apparently characterized by acquisitive and competitive patterns. For them it was desirable to be regarded as "big men" with many dependents, to enjoy *kpatei* (Mende for "richness" or "worth"), and to receive *matei* ("food for

---

[9] The distinction of town and village society was made by Little, 1967, pp. 103-08.
[10] On pragmatism see Little, 1954, pp. 112-13. On secrecy, see Little, 1967, p. 8.

our parents") from dependent villagers. In turn the townsmen protected the dependents, settled disputes for them and satisfied other obligations. Also, fruits of political office were vigorously contested by the town elite.

In addition, the town folk were the first to be engaged by social, political and commercial aspects of the superimposed Western social system. Thus, historical circumstance made it possible for townfolk to transpose traditional patterns of competition and acquisition into the Western framework of stipends, salaries, commissions and mission education. This transposition followed the lines of the reciprocity relationship modeled by the nineteenth century new rulers.

Villagers were committed to obedience and subsistence. They traditionally looked to the townsmen as parental figures, for the resolution of disputes and for legal and military protection. Also, villagers lived according to a "subsistence ethic" in which necessities, but not large accumulations of property, were produced. By virtue of their particular social and economic patterns, as well as by their relative physical isolation from continuous contact with modernizing agencies, village society tended to continue for a time along its own lines. There was a time lag between the response of townsfolk and that of village folk to the impact of the West.

It is my thesis that Christianity was transformed in Kori and Bumpe chiefdoms along two lines in interaction with the town and village strata within the total context of the modernization process.

IV

The first line of transformation was related to the townsfolk. Mission institutions, especially schools, were utilized by them for the transposition of traditional goals into the modern sector. The institutional religious concomitant was the emergence of "town Christianity."

Beginning in 1900 primary schools were maintained under UMC administrative arrangements in both Rotifunk and Taiama, as well as in outlying centers in the chiefdoms. In addition to academic instruction, Taiama (as well as Rotifunk in the earlier years) was notable for its stress on light industrial education. In 1936, Charles Leader reported from Taiama, "Our industrial program has been enlarged during the year and now in addition to Agriculture, Building, some Blacksmithing, we have the making of Native Furniture and Tailoring.'' [11]

Boarding homes were attached to the schools at Rotifunk (until 1939) and Taiama. In addition, interested Africans associated with the school and church often opened their homes to boarders.

Many paramount chiefs of the two chiefdoms cooperated with the mission in the support of schools and the recruitment of scholars. For instance, in 1921 Chief Morlu Briwah of Kori chiefdom, perhaps at the suggestion of missionaries and certainly after consultation with his headmen, conscripted scholars into the Taiama UBC school by assigning quotas to each section of the chiefdom.[12] The conscription resulted in 45 new scholars, for whom the chiefdom provided food. Similar arrangements lasted until 1925.[13] Among the chiefs of Bumpe, the notable leader in educational endeavors was A. G. Caulker, who supported many boys in school and even underwrote the entire operating expenses of a UBC primary school in Bumpe Town for many years.

Some chiefs, notably A. G. Caulker, supported mission schools because the development of Christian character through education was important to them. Caulker and others also felt that only through formal education could their people prepare themselves to deal with the development of the country. Further, traditional rivalries between ruling families were sometimes projected into the educational sphere so that various ruling houses competed for openings and in acquiring schools for their section towns. The latter was particularly true of the Caulker and Fosana families, leading to the establishment of primary schools at Bumpe Town (the Caulker town) and Yenkissa (the Fosana town) in Bumpe Chiefdom.

Government also supported mission schools. Even before the 1898 White Man's War, Governor Cardew made provision for some small disbursements to mission schools, but regular financial support began in 1910 through a grants scheme.[14]

---

[11] Leader, 1936, p. 79.

[12] Morlu Briwah was a son of M'biriwa, cited in Chapter Three as following within the "new ruler" pattern.

[13] Reeck, 1971, Interviews No. 32, Taiama, Kori Chiefdom, p. 211; No. 60, Waiima, Kori Chiefdom, p. 361; and No. 72, Vaama, Kori Chiefdom, p. 476.

[14] SLA, Governor (Probyn), Despatch No. 337/1910 to Secretary of State (Crewe), pp. 3-4.

The schools, then, functioned as instruments of the modernizing intentions of the government and chiefs as well as of the intent of the missionaries to develop a cadre of Westernized Africans capable of sustaining a church organization on the UBC American model. The schools became a focus of the continuing reciprocity relationship first noticed in Chapter Two. But what were the effects of schooling on the social mobilization process?

A measure of social mobilization related to attendance at Taiama and Rotifunk schools is suggested by data collected on five groups of scholars. These scholars were listed as passing annual exams at Rotifunk in 1904, 1924 and 1934, and at Taiama in years 1925 and 1934. The data were gathered in interviews with informants having memories of those years.

First, school attendance was associated closely with urbanization. Of 89 scholars whose home towns could be determined (out of a sample of 105), 81 (91 %) sprang from villages or second-class towns (chiefdom headquarters) and only 8 (9 %) came from first-class towns (mining and commercial centers such as Tongo Fields, Yengemah, Bo and Moyamba) or urban areas (Freetown). For the same scholars, of 77 whose working residence was determined, only 25 (31 %) lived in villages or second-class towns whereas 52 (69 %) were in large towns, urban areas or abroad.

Likewise, occupational mobility was a phenomenon associated with school attendance. Of 85 of the same sample of scholars whose family backgrounds were ascertained, 43 (51 %) had fathers who could be classified in the traditional sector (village farmers or traditional ruling strata). But of 78 whose occupational career was reported, only 10 (13 %) fell into the traditional category whereas the remainder (87 %) worked in the modern sector, with the largest number in labor or trade classifications and smaller numbers in professional or supervisory capacities. (To divide this sample into traditional and modern categories is not to suggest that all particular individuals were either traditional or modern, which would be patent nonsense, but rather to use somewhat arbitrary indices to display the social change associated with schooling.)

As to the sources of these recruits, of the 43 whose fathers were classified as traditional, 24 were children of officeholders or traditional ruling elite, whereas only 19 came from strictly village agricultural families. Of course, in both chiefdoms village farmers formed the great bulk of the population pyramid. Numerous statements from both villagers and the educated support the contention that the traditional town elite in Kori and Bumpe chiefdoms was the main source of scholars.[15] Villagers spoke of hiding their children in the bush to evade school recruiters. The masses resisted schooling because children were needed in farm work and because they feared to send their offspring away from the village to the boarding home in the hands of whites. Hence, it appears that the traditional townfolk were the more adaptive to opportunities of formal schooling, although it would be misleading to suggest either that all families in the towns supported schooling or that all persons in the village stratum were completely resistant.

Another indication of the importance of the schools for social mobilization and political modernization is the significant number of mission-associated Africans who became involved in protectorate and national politics and administration. For instance, one of the antecedents of the Sierra Leone People's Party was the Sierra Leone Organization Society (SOS), founded in 1946. Kilson names six founders of the SOS.[16] Three of the six were onetime employees of the UMC as teachers; one was a UMC clergyman; and one was an M.D. and clergyman employed at one time by the Rotifunk Hospital. It appears probable from informal information that all five of these had been UMC scholars, although documentary evidence is not available. The Paramount Chief of Bumpe, A. G. Caulker, who in 1943 became one of the first two protectorate Africans to sit on the Executive Council of the Legislative Council, was a graduate of the Shenge UMC school.[17] "Old boys" of Rotifunk and Taiama have become ministers of the national government, ambassadors and administrators as well as union leaders, workers and members of several professions.

That so many of their scholars abandoned careers in the church and took up nonecclesiastical work surprised missionaries. As one veteran missionary of Rotifunk told me, "Way back, I would say in the 'twenties or 'thirties, people did think that it wasn't quite cricket to be trained in the mission and go off to the government." [18] While many contemporary missionaries would point to this record

---

[15] This is consistent with Kilson, 1966, pp. 53-67, where it is noted that the modernizing elite emerged, in the main, from the traditional elite.

[16] Kilson, 1966, p. 229.

[17] Kilson, 1966, p. 143.

[18] Reeck, 1971, Interview No. 4, Dayton, Ohio, p. 13.

of training for secular leadership with considerable satisfaction, for those of the first half of the twentieth century the secular aspect of social mobilization via mission schools was quite unintentional.

Missionaries organized socially mobilized Christian converts into church congregations in both Kori and Bumpe chiefdoms. "Town Christianity" is a term I will use to refer to patterns of Christian practice and organization characteristic of the modernizing sector.

Due to its suitable location for trade, Rotifunk had a sizable Creole population, especially during the first five or six decades of the twentieth century. The mission congregation there was supported by the participation of Creoles and modernizing Sherbro, Lokko and Temne people. A study of social characteristics of seventy-three contributors to the church fund in the years 1900, 1909 and 1934 shows that 96 per cent were engaged in occupations in the modern sector of the economy and 51 per cent were Creole. Despite attempts to enlist illiterates from time to time the Rotifunk congregation was almost totally identified with literate and modernizing persons and remains so today.

In Kori Chiefdom a high percentage of Africans participating in the modern sector of the economy (teachers, traders, administrators and mission employees) were baptized and professed UMC members. The large church building, with its seating capacity of more than a thousand, was the location of worship services. In 1969, attendance on the Sundays of my visits averaged about three hundred. About half of those in attendance were school children under some compulsion. Sunday and weekday evening prayer services had much lower attendances.

The Sunday service was patterned on the American EUB-UMC model, with the use of English language, singing accompanied by organ to hymns chosen from the EUB Hymnal and both spontaneous and formal prayers. The service was dominated by the preacher and his assistant through the lengthy sermon, announcements and short discourses concerning offerings and church manners.

Among the teachers, traders and other subelite that participated in the congregational life, one found a small core characterized by a high rate of participation. The majority, however, participated in worship and other meetings occasionally and did not faithfully observe many of the behavioral standards enjoined by traditional church discipline, such as abstention from tobacco and alcohol. It appeared that many of the subelite preferred to pour their energies

into chiefdom politics, family affairs and occupational life rather
than into church life.

From the missionary point of view, the failure of town Christianity
was that it had fallen so far short of the goal of ecclesiastical regularization. On the other hand it did embody some patterns of Westernization valued by the missionaries. The mission was valued by the town-
people, I feel, more because it had been the sponsor of means for
transposition into the modernizing sector than for its worship life.
Great resentment was felt by the elites (modernizing and traditional)
over recent annual decreases in subsidies from America to the
boarding home and the hospital, whereas the decreasing church
attendance did not seem to arouse similar concern.

In summary, mission-sponsored schools maintained by missionaries
led to the development of a literate, self-supporting cadre of churchmen
and were used by Africans, particularly the townspeople, as a means
of access to opportunities in the modern sector. The result was the
formation of a modernizing elite and subelite, characterized by
literacy, occupational and geographical mobility and formal adherence
to The United Methodist Church. The corresponding pattern of
Christian practice, called "town Christianity," was quite devoid of
rigid ecclesiastical standards formerly enjoined by missionaries. The
regard of townspeople for the church seemed to arise from its social
benefits.

In the historical process of the building of the religious institutions,
a transformation occurred so that "town Christianity" was not
identical with the missionary goals for the African church. Instead,
a new pattern emerged, not anticipated by the missionary vision
of Christianity. Likewise, the recruitment of persons from the traditional elite into mission institutions was explained on the basis of
traditional commitments to acquisition and competition. Traditional
commitments were transposed into a new institutional framework
along the lines of the reciprocity pattern. Thus, if social mobilization
is meaningful in the context of Kori and Bumpe chiefdoms, it is
in the sense that persons from the ruling stratum were capable of
adapting their traditional commitments to newly emergent structural
settings grounded in the interplay of African and Western forces
but not entirely anticipated in either. If the townspeople were modern-
ized, the church was at the same time traditionalized.

V

Village Christianity is the second of the two fairly distinct patterns of Christian religious practice within the UMC in Kori Chiefdom. Since widespread village Christianity never emerged in Bumpe Chiefdom, due largely to the neglect of intensive itineration there during the twentieth century, this section refers only to Kori.

Village Christians belong to the large population base living in villages outside of Taiama. The rate of adherence to Christianity among villagers is perhaps 50 per cent of the total population or more, a remarkably high rate for Sierra Leone. On the whole, village Christians are illiterate, though some have attained a degree of literacy in Mende and fewer in English through church literacy classes.

Many of the villages of the chiefdom have a worship leader and Christian worship services. The goal set by the town pastor is a service every week in each village, but the frequency varies from village to village depending on the size of the Christian group, the vigor of the leader and the degree of support he is able to enlist.

Services in the villages differ in several respects from those in the town. The linguistic medium is Mende instead of English. The meetings may be held on the veranda of a leading person, in the village barri (shelter for communal meetings) or in a thatch church if one has been constructed. There is generally little or no preaching, but prayers are said and many songs are sung. The singing, instead of in Western hymn form, is generally in the traditional Mende mode led by a precentor, who calls out a line to which the rest respond. Holy communion and baptism are never to my knowledge celebrated in village congregations, whereas the town church enjoys a full sacramental life.

The town and the village congregations are organized into the Taiama UMC Parish. According to information supplied by the pastor's assistant in 1969, there are 97 villages with congregations. The 97 villages are grouped into 16 geographical sections, each with a section leader. The 16 sections are subsidiary to the Taiama church and pastor, so in the final analysis the educated townspeople have authority over the village congregations, just as townspeople had authority over villagers in traditional society.

A demonstration of unity between village congregations and the town church is that villagers often walk to the Taiama church for services, especially on festival occasions, when reportedly the atten-

dance has reached as high as 1,500. To accommodate both villagers
and townspeople, Taiama worship services are really two services
compacted into one. Despite the fact that virtually all worshippers
understand Mende, English language prayers, songs and sermons
are provided for scholars, teachers and others of the modernizing
sector, while Mende prayers, songs and exhortations are inserted
for walkers from the villages. Mende songs in this case, however,
are ordinarily printed in a Mende hymnal and sung with organ
accompaniment to Western tunes.

An interpretation of the social factors leading to the development
of village Christianity might best begin with the observation that
its emergence, like that of town Christianity but in a different way,
only partly fulfilled the missionary model. Village Christianity successfully fulfilled the universalization goal, but neither the ecclesiastical
regularization nor the Westernization aspects, of the missionary
model. On the other hand, village Christianity represented from the
Mende perspective a domestication of missionary Christianity to a
point where its acceptance was not threatening to village social
patterns inherited from earlier generations. Village Christianity acts
as a shock absorber against the impact of the West.

The peasant masses resisted conversion almost unitedly until
about 1940. With their subsistence agricultural patterns, missionary
Christianity had less to offer them than it offered to the townsfolk.
However, when the parish came under the management of Pastor
B. A. Carew, the village masses began to swell the church rolls,
primarily because they related to Carew as to a traditional "big
man."

In effect, Carew built up a new social subsystem in the Taiama
Parish, patterned along traditional lines.[19] Just as familial, political
and secret society bonds converged from the villages upon elders
or "big men" in Taiama, so did the Taiama Parish as it developed
around Carew. When he visited in the villages he consoled people
in their own language. When they walked to Taiama on Sundays
he fed them, just as "big men" are expected to be hospitable to
village relatives and dependents. In addition, Carew's positions of
responsibility in the Sierra Leone UMC Conference and his international travel to general conferences of the UMC further enhanced
his status in the eyes of villagers (as well as in those of the modernizing

---

[19] Olson, 1969, p. 159, confirms this judgment.

group). In short, Carew became a very "big man" in Taiama during
his long tenure, and it was his organizational skill, hard work and
dispensation of tangible and intangible rewards along traditional
lines that account in large part for the growth of the church in Kori
villages.

Another important factor in the adherence of the masses to Christianity was the service of two blind itinerants, Pa Mbovai and Matthew
Moamie. I was not able to establish exact dates, but Mbovai was
active as early as 1925 and Matthew as late as 1954. Village informants
were imbued with memories of these blind evangelists — how they
memorized and repeated whole sections of the Bible, how they made
their way alone about the difficult paths between villages and how
they sang. Both men were prolific in the composition of Christian
songs in Mende mode, sung and loved still in village churches. There
was even the suggestion that these men were respected in part for
their "powers" or magical ability, indicated by their moving about
from place to place and by their "reading from the Book," though
blind.

Certainly there were additional factors accounting for the adherence
to Christianity by the masses, such as respect for Charles Leader
(a "big man" in his own right) and appreciation of the power appre-
hended in the medicine of the mission clinic. But in emphasizing
the manner in which B. A. Carew and the blind evangelists presented
institutional Christianity in ways consistent with the traditional
patterns of subsistence, awe and dependence characteristic of the
masses, I have touched on those factors that have come to account
most fully in my mind for the transformation of missionary Christianity
into village Christianity.

Among village Christians the old Mende *rites de passage* and other
institutions such as secret societies, ancestor veneration, polygyny,
communal life and the subsistence economic ethic remain virtually
intact, in addition to all of which has been superadded some aspects
of Christian belief and practice : a heightened awareness of God
(*ngewo*), assistance through prayer in practical encounters with harm
and danger and fellowship or sociability. (A town Christian who
was a trained social scientist told me that the best contribution of
Christianity to village life had been increased and regular sociability,
as compared to the seasonal sociability of the secret societies.) [20]

---

[20] Reeck, 1971, Interview No. 97, Taiama, Kori Chiefdom, pp. 654-55.

Evidently Carew's great drive for universal adherence made it virtually impossible to enforce strict standards among the village converts, so that the practice of many features of Mende life supposedly proscribed by church discipline was simply taken for granted by village Christians at the time of my field work.

In short, both townsmen and villagers selected aspects of missionary Christianity that were compatible with inherited patterns. As a result, the imported missionary model of Christianity was transformed and traditionalized, some Mende values were expressed through this transformed institution, and the African church that came into existence was a novel emergence in Mende-Sherbro social history.

The configuration of religious patterns in the chiefdoms was in flux in 1969. B. A. Carew had left his position at Taiama to assume an administrative position in Freetown and the UMC organization was eroding because his successor was not his equal as a "big man" and did not command sufficient resources to enable him to feed villagers after church on Sunday. The itineration system had virtually collapsed. Church attendance was in decline and parish organization was weakening.

For the first time the UMC was faced with serious competition from other Christian bodies. A priest was saying Mass on Sundays for a small group of Roman Catholics. But a greater threat was posed by the American-supported Church of Christ. Subsidized by funds from the outside, in 1968 a young elder began recruiting whole UMC village congregations into this sect through the preaching of withdrawal from the "apostate" UMC and, quite significantly, through entertaining villagers with feasts. The pastor and other UMC leaders were finding difficulty in enforcing loyalty in the face of this competitive approach.

At the same time Islam seemed to be resurgent. A new cement block mosque and school complex was under construction in a conspicuous place in Taiama, bound to usurp the visual prominence of the church building upon completion.

Likewise in Rotifunk the Roman Catholic Church and Muslims were advancing organizationally and building new facilities, although the UMC was not faced by sectarian protest from the Church of Christ there.

Given the continuance of Mende-Sherbro pragmatism in matters of religion, the short-term future would undoubtedly see the development of a new Christian pluralism and a relative increase in Muslim influence.

VI

I do not deny that important institutional changes, such as social mobilization and the technical equipment of persons to participate in new occupations, took place in Kpaa-Mende and Sherbro societies under the impact of missionary activity within the context of colonial modernization. I do, however, question any theoretical schemes that simplify the process into a discrete transition from traditional to modern outlooks and institutions.

It strikes me as important that although missionary Christianity implied thoroughgoing change in the first instance, it was itself "traditionalized" through African participation into town Christianity and village Christianity. Out of the framework of their received values, both townspeople and villagers were able to "domesticate" the incoming institutions for local participation.

In view of this, the main suggestion to be derived from this study for modernization theory is that no clear distinction between traditional and modern exists in the historical process of interaction between Mende and Western societies, and that the concepts "traditional" and "modern" should be used as ideal types to organize complex data.[21] Things for the Kpaa Mende hardly fell apart under Western influence. African traditional society proved itself perfectly capable of adapting to and mastering external threats to its fundamental forms of existence.

---

[21] I am impressed with the similarity between these conclusions and those drawn by Singer, 1971, from studies in Indian society.

CHAPTER FIVE

ISLAM IN KORI CHIEFDOM

It is sometimes asserted that major proportions of indigenous populations in forest areas in West Africa are in the process of conversion from traditional religious practices and beliefs to Islam. In this chapter I wish to show how questions arise concerning that assertion through the analysis of the past century of Muslim life in the Kori Chiefdom in Sierra Leone. Through distinguishing emergent patterns of Islam and relating these patterns to each other and to the broader historical process a basis will be made for the suggestion that Islam has been assimilated by the Mende in a way that calls into question the assertion noted above.

The chapter is organized around a hypothesis that all Muslims in the nineteenth century were regarded by Mende as strangers and were welcome in the chiefdom because they offered techniques for linking the Mende to external sources of certain desired values. There were two types of Islam. One type of Islam offered techniques to acquire "force" in the spiritual-cultural realm. The other type initially had little to do with Mende culture, but its adherents inter-posed in the economic realm between the agriculturalist Mende and external trade centers. Further, as both types perpetuated themselves and recruited adherents from Mende society, Islam in the chiefdom can still today be understood as of two fairly distinct types: "Stranger Islam," small numerically, the members of which supply economic services, and "Mende Islam," which can be understood as consisting of technical additions to the traditional Mende repertory of means for dealing with *halei* for its many adherents.[1]

Halei is the generally latent force that, in the Mende consciousness of reality, impregnates the universe and is the basis of the efficacy of instruments and techniques employed to secure supernatural ends. Mende society supports technicians or specialists in the use

---

[1] The procedure of analyzing Maliki Islam in West Africa into two types is common. Trimingham, 1961, distinguished Muslim traditionalism from neo-Islam. Fisher, 1968, distinguished reforming from acclimatized Islam.

of *halei* including officials of the secret societies and private practitioners.[2]

Kori Chiefdom has a current population of about twenty thousand, consisting largely of farmers who live in small villages scattered throughout the chiefdom. The two large centers are the chief town of Taiama and Njala University College. Njala is located near the southern boundary of the chiefdom and has not until quite recently significantly affected the patterns of Islam in the chiefdom. Taiama, however, has long been influential for the development of Islam. Taiama is the trade, political and educational center of the chiefdom, with a current population of about two thousand. It was a focal point in the Kpaa Mende migration of earlier centuries. In the nineteenth century Taiama was a strongly fortified town and was said to have been the capital of the entire Kpaa Mende region from the Gorama Mende Chiefdom in the East to Senehun on the Bumpe River in the West.

With this introduction we can proceed to analyze the emergent patterns of Islam in Kori Chiefdom in the late nineteenth century to date.

I

Muslim patterns in the nineteenth century are partly, perhaps largely, to be understood as functions of Mende needs growing out of the intertribal conflicts and the impact of the West.

The influence of Freetown as a center of commerce increased during the nineteenth century in the Taiama area, particularly late in the century. European trade firms established "factories" or trade centers at the navigable heads of rivers north and south of Freetown. Trade centers that particularly influenced Taiama Mende were located at Waterloo, Rotifunk and Senehun/Bumpe. Trade and diplomatic interchange between Taiama Mende and the West took place at the ports named, particularly at Senehun. Visits by Creole itinerant traders and by government agents to Taiama were unusual before the 1890s. In the absence of the direct presence of Western forces in Taiama a trade mechanism emerged to link the Mende agriculturalists with the West.

---

[2] Paraphrased from Little, 1967, pp. 227-28. The terms "Stranger Islam" and "Mende Islam" will be developed throughout the chapter. They represent what I observed to be two types of Islam in Kori Chiefdom.

Even prior to this linking of the commercial forces of the West with Taiama Mende, an overland trade existed between the North and Taiama, the imports consisting, apparently, largely of cattle and the exports consisting largely of slaves.[3] This trade was brought to Taiama by Mandingo, Susu and Fula traders, who appear to have resided for considerable lengths of time in Taiama under the protection of the chief and with a landlord while negotiating the exchange of goods. These strangers were Muslim but apparently had no permanent mosque. What was the nature of the Islam they followed ? It is assumed that their original homelands were in regions influenced by the theocratic states of the Fouta Jallon. If so, they must have understood the notion of the sovereignty of God in human affairs.

In response to the growing attraction of Western commerce in the 1860s and 1870s the strangers from the North, who had taken up residence in Taiama, began to develop the routes linking Taiama to Senehun/Bumpe (the town of Gbanyah and Madam Yoko), Rotifunk and Waterloo. Though some Mende certainly walked down to trade centers, in general the Mende were reluctant to engage in the overland march for several reasons.

Thus, Muslim strangers played a large part in developing and maintaining trade links between the Mende in and around Taiama and two external markets : first, markets for domestic slaves in the North, probably at least as far as the Fouta Jallon; and second, centers related to Western commercial interests at riverheads to the West. These traders were the earliest source for the development of the Stranger type of Islam.[4]

The earliest basis for the development of a second type of Islam among the Mende of Taiama grew out of the practice followed by leading warriors and chiefs of including in their retinue Muslim Mandingo and Susu workers of supernatural means.[5] The way in which the Mende saw them using symbols of Islam as means for channeling *halei* to assure victory was entirely compatible with traditional Mende notions of cause and effect. As such, Islam seems merely to have been added extrinsically to the Mende repertory

---

[3] Reeck, 1971, Interview No. 93, Taiama, Kori Chiefdom, p. 609; and No. 75, Taiama, pp. 515-17.

[4] Many observers have noted the important role played by traders in the spread of Islam. See Trimingham and Fyfe, 1960, pp. 36-37, and Hopewell, 1958.

[5] See, for example, Reeck, 1971, Interview No. 72, Vaama, Kori Chiefdom, p. 474.

of means for accomplishing certain ends.[6] The employment of a Muslim as a worker in *halei* certainly did not imply any exclusive commitment to Islam as a way of life with a locus of authority transcending Mende culture. Rather, aspects of Islam seem to have been subsumed into the Mende world view as a practical measure — hence, "Mende Islam."

By virtue of association with civil and war chiefs, Islam undoubtedly acquired considerable prestige with the masses. Furthermore, trust relationships were established between Mende leaders and Muslim advisers.[7] These factors seem to have readied the chiefdom for a widespread utilitarian acceptance of Islam in the twentieth century, and thus the workers in supernatural means, though not themselves of the Mende tribe, can be regarded as a significant source of the Mende type of Islam.

During the nineteenth century, as we have seen, the roots of Islam were sent down among the Taiama Mende.[8] The Islam of this period can be understood as already having consisted of two types: first, relatively normative Maliki Islam, practiced by stranger traders; second, the use of Islamic symbols as means by practitioners within the limits of the Mende conceptions of cause and effect, for Mende purposes.

II

In the twentieth century the Muslim influence continued to develop and expand along the lines begun in the nineteenth.

Certain social developments occurred among the Stranger Muslim type. The demise of warfare enforced by colonial controls led to a slackening of demand for the services of workers of means. No longer needed in the chiefs' courts, Muslims continued to work means

---

[6] This jugment is supported by information from Little, 1967, p. 229, where he includes the *mori*-man as one among several types of medicine man or workers in *halei*. I prefer the term "Muslim workers in supernatural means" to *mori*-man because in Kori Chiefdom *mori*-man seems to have been understood as any Muslim, worker in means or not.

[7] A leading Muslim of the Mende type, converted about 1915, said, "The reason why we believed in the teaching of Islam — because when our ancestors were warriors the *Mori*-men used to work for them to be successful. So therefore [we] had every cause to hold a firm belief in Islam." Reeck, 1971, Interview No. 67, Taiama, Kori Chiefdom, p. 419.

[8] This is not to imply that Islam was not present earlier.

privately, selling amulets or phylacteries to individual Mende. The number of such practitioners in Taiama today is only three or four and they are not highly regarded by many of the Stranger Muslim type.[9]

As elsewhere in West Africa during this period, however, Muslim traders were strengthened in their position through the imposition of colonial control of the hinterland, made effective in Kori Chiefdom shortly after the British victory of 1898. The colonial government sought, as we have seen, to expand trade and to increase the commercialization of hinterland life. The factory system spread inland along waterways and along the railroad. The rail passed along the southern boundary of Kori Chiefdom and intersected the Taia [Teye] River downstream about twenty miles from Taiama at Mano. Trade firms managed by Creoles, expatriates and Lebanese, sprouted up shortly after 1900 at Mano, later at Taiama. Manufactured goods came up the river from Mano in canoes and boats for sale in Taiama; produce was gathered in Taiama and sent down to Mano for transshipment to Freetown on the rail. Taking advantage of openings in the new commercial life, the Muslim sons of the nineteenth century traders evolved between 1900 and 1970 from tailors to traders, contractors and entrepreneurs.

The mosque emerged as a social institution shortly after 1900. A mosque building was constructed at an early date, probably about 1903, upon the suggestion of Madam Yoko, the powerful chief of the Kpaa Mende Chiefdom. (Kori Chiefdom was formed out of the Kpaa Mende Chiefdom when the latter broke up in 1919 after the death of Madam Yoko.) The organizer of the construction appears to have been a Mende (though not a native of Taiama) by the name of Vandy, a leader in Taiama politics and at one point a chiefdom speaker.[10] The Muslim Strangers who supported the mosque were able, apparently at least as early as 1916, to support an Alimamy ("Alimamy" is the colloquial for Imam) and a Koranic teacher.[11] "Big Muslims," all strangers from the North, formed the core of the Muslim social organization. The authority of the Alimamy to judge disputes between Muslims according to Islamic law came to be accepted by the chiefs.

---

[9] Reeck, 1971, Interview No. 48, Taiama, Kori Chiefdom, p. 304.

[10] Reeck, 1971, Interview No. 49, Taiama, Kori Chiefdom, pp. 319-20.

[11] Reeck, 1971, Interview No. 44, Taiama, Kori Chiefdom, pp. 275-78; No. 49, Taiama, p. 321; and No. 75, Taiama, pp. 518-19.

The present Alimamy is considered to have jurisdiction over cases that arise between Muslims. If the case cannot be settled within the Muslim community, it is referred to the local court.[12] The Alimamy is accustomed to asking two of the elders of the mosque to consult with him in hearing disputes.

The Stranger Muslims in Taiama itself, consisting of about ten nuclear families of Mandingo, Susu and Fula, maintain a close group identity and a sense of community.[13] They are each others' frequent companions. In the evening the men can be observed gathering on verandahs near the mosque for a friendly chat before or after prayers. Their group identity is enhanced by the many characteristics they have in common as dictinct from the Mende culture around them.

Insofar as chiefdom political life is concerned the Stranger Muslims have virtually no direct influence over it and no aspiration to office. (The late Vandy, mentioned earlier, was an exception to the typology being developed because he was a leader in the mosque but also a Mende and a political figure.) They have no claims to high office partly because they lack the ability to demonstrate descent from a chiefdom founder, a *sine qua non* for the office of paramount chief in the practical workings of politics.[14]

In the social sphere, links have been made between the Stranger Muslims and some Mende families through marriage. The earliest traders appear to have come as bachelors and to have made arrangements for Mende women to be their wives.[15] The contemporary Stranger Muslims descend from these marriages. In such marriages

---

[12] Reeck, 1971, Interview No. 75, Taiama, Kori Chiefdom, p. 519. My impression is that cases are judged only infrequently by the Alimamy. Considering the large number of Muslims in the chiefdom, the infrequency of cases coming before the Alimamy seems to suggest that the large percentage of disputes between Muslims, at least of the Mende type, are taken directly to the chief and that the Alimamy is bypassed. If so, the legal ethos of the Mende Muslims would clearly be the traditional Mende notions.

[13] Temne in Kori Chiefdom who are Muslim deserve attention but are excluded from the present study because they seem to be highly impermanent residents and have not formed structural relationships to Mende society nor to the Stranger Muslims as defined above.

[14] In national politics M.P.s are elected from constituencies. M.P.s appear to often utilize secret societies as bases for political strength. Stranger Muslims have no access to this base. This may help explain why Islam has not been a strong factor in internal political life in the Mende areas of Sierra Leone. For a different view and a broader perspective see Trimingham, 1966, p. 306.

[15] Reeck, 1971, Interview No. 75, Taiama, Kori Chiefdom, p. 515.

the wife's identity appears to be centered about the husband and his family, however, and is thus oriented much more to the patterns of Stranger Islam and the mosque than to the wife's parents' culture. It is through the sons and daughters of such marriages that growth has come to the Stranger Muslim type.[16]

Secret societies have traditionally acted as fundamental unifying and controlling agencies in Mende society and, in frequently unobtrusive ways, still do. Stranger Islam, however, is unrelated to the secret societies. The leading Stranger Muslim males do not belong to the male societies (Poro and Wunde), they remember their fathers as not wanting society membership, and the Alimamy preaches against secret society membership in the mosque. The Alimamy objects to "...secret arrangements whereby people pray to objects in the form of *baal* and then make a big feast in their honor..." and sees such activity as indication of devotion to a second god.[17]

In moving to consider the growth of the Mende type of Islam, as indicated above, during the present century, a very large number of Mende (perhaps three thousand in the chiefdom, though this is only a very rough estimate) have adhered to Islam particularly as a result of the preaching of traveling prophets, "evangelists" and village prayer leaders.[18] Mende Muslims can be distinguished from Stranger Muslims by several criteria. Occupationally the Mende Muslims find livelihood largely in agricultural and political pursuits. (A number of twentieth century paramount chiefs have sympathized with or adhered to Islam, including the incumbent.) Another difference, more fundamental, involves the fact that Mende Muslims adhere to secret societies. One informant stated, "Secret societies were traditions, so whether a Muslim or a Christian we still have to follow our tradition by getting membership to our secret societies." There is evidence that even village prayer leaders who could be classified as Muslims of the Mende type were "society men." [19]

---

[16] For example see Reeck, 1971, Interview No. 94, Taiama, Kori Chiefdom, p. 624.

[17] See Reeck, 1971, Interviews No. 44, Taiama, Kori Chiefdom, p. 276 and No. 75, Taiama, pp. 517, 519-20.

[18] Itinerant preachers appear to have been and to still be quite common in Kori Chiefdom. For an anthropologist's description of the activity of such a person see Little, 1946, pp. 111-13.

[19] See Reeck, 1971, Interview No. 68, Taninahun, Kori Chiefdom, p. 428; and No. 76, Fogbo, Kori Chiefdom, p. 551.

The fact of secret society membership suggests that Islam has been assimilated on a very selective basis by a proportion of the masses. The sacrifices, processions, prayers and other symbols that have been assimilated seem to be compatible with the Mende concept of the manipulation of *halei* for social health and personal well-being.[20] Islam of the Mende Muslim type appears not to threaten the traditional Mende worldview. Thus it is apparent that the Islam of the Mende Muslim type of the twentieth century bears roughly the same relationship to Mende cosmology as that of the Muslim workers of supernatural means bore in the nineteenth century. The addition of elements of Islam may not, even over the long haul, lead to the disintegration of the traditional Mende fundamental religious beliefs.

Villagers of the Mende Muslim type have certain obligations to the mosque in Taiama that bring them into association with the Stranger Muslims. Some villagers walk to Taiama for Friday prayers and festivals. The elders of the Taiama mosque (Stranger Muslims) call on villagers for financial assistance in projects such as the construction of the new mosque (under way in 1968-69). Evidence indicates, however, that the authority of the Stranger Muslims controlling the mosque over Mende Muslims rarely extends to the religio-legal elements of Islam. Villagers of the Mende Muslim type have not come under the control of the Alimamy nor of the Law and do not, apparently, care to submit to either.

Thus Islam and Muslims are valued by Mende for limited reasons. The Stranger Muslims have had a part in maintaining trade relations with the West; they are valued for their role in trade but not necessarily for their relatively normative Islam. But the Mende masses have incorporated technical aspects of Islam which they have come to appreciate into their own religious beliefs, sometimes in place of some of their original practices, though not to an extent that would threaten their fundamental traditional religio-cultural notions. Rather, it is due to these very notions that they have been able to value technical aspects of Islam as practically beneficial.

---

[20] If further investigation confirms this tentative conclusion even God would be a secondary or instrumental concern, and petitions to him might be for purposes of manipulation, not of submission, for Muslims of the Mende type.

III

Two special matters deserve detailed discussion : Stranger Muslims as entrepreneurs and the case of the Wali-yu.

At the turn of the century the Muslims of the Stranger type were mostly tailors but over the years have developed several kinds of business enterprises. At the time of this research the little group of Stranger Muslims dominated certain activities in the modern economic sector and competed in others. For instance, one operated the only *poda poda* (small intercity transport bus) running from Taiama.[21] The same individual operated the only rice mill in the chiefdom. Another owned the best rental residential property in Taiama and had developed a small but well stocked retail shop. This was the only African-operated shop in Taiama in position to compete with Lebanese shops in selling Western goods. The same individual had entered production agriculture through the raising of chickens and turkeys, processing and freezing them and selling them through supermarkets in Freetown. Another family operated the chiefdom's only petrol station, located at Mokunde on the Freetown-Bo road. Others engaged in the more traditional forms of produce and goods trade, though one of these had formerly contracted for certain construction projects in the chiefdom. These activities require capital and management. In this connection many of the Stranger Muslims utilized banking services.

Opportunities presented by the modern economic forces impinging on Kori Chiefdom have been entered virtually as a group by those of the Stranger Muslim type. Rather than merely mediating between the commercial West and the Mende agricultural economy, however, the emphasis seems to be shifting to positive embodiment of the notions of rationalization, entrepreneurship, profit seeking and capital formation, once identified as Western. Reasons for this shift may include the inability of this group to compete politically, their freedom from certain Mende obligations and attitudes and their accumulation of skills and experience in the matters of trade and financial endeavor. These Stranger Muslims have been able to turn themselves into virtually the only African representatives of the

---

[21] In reference to this service and others following it is recognized that Njala University College also operates such services but only for the use of persons connected with the institution.

"Protestant Ethic" in Kori Chiefdom. The notion of the function of Muslims of this type as interposers between the Western economic patterns and Mende agriculturalists appears valid for the twentieth century as well as the nineteenth, and their Stranger community has been supported and shaped through the performance of this role.

Another matter to be discussed is the incident of the visit to Kori Chiefdom in 1916 of the Wali-yu. Wali-yu is a colloquialism used in reference to a type of prophet called *Wali* in Arabic.[22] Despite a detailed search of government archives and mission periodicals only two written references clearly related to the Wali-yu could be located. One was a comment by a district commissioner concerning a dispute between the Wali-yu and the paramount chief of Yonni Chiefdom and the other was a deprecatory remark by a missionary.[23] The absence of written commentary falls short of signifying the vast influence of the Wali-yu on the chiefdom at the time of his visit. In tours to towns surrounding Taiama and during his stay in Taiama itself he influenced hundreds, perhaps thousands, in favor of Islam. Many informants said that conversions were encouraged by threats that any who refused would be turned to stones or other objects. The Wali-yu ministered in Taiama with the permission of the chief, but excesses of the Wali-yu against secret societies caused the chief eventually to ask him to leave the chiefdom. It is said that the Wali-yu exposed the Poro devil in the middle of town and entered the Bundu bush to scatter the initiates. In addition the Wali-yu recruited a number of scholars from among the leading families and instructed them in Islam. These scholars left the chiefdom with the Wali-yu and, oral information has it, accompanied him south to Liberia. In Liberia apparently the Wali-yu was arrested and extradited to Sierra Leone.[24] Several of the young scholars returned home to Kori Chiefdom and have remained attached to Islam.

---

[22] A *wali* is a kind of local saint or miracle-worker. See Gibb and Kramer, 1953, pp. 629-30. The Wali-yu was probably a far-roving *marabout*, as he was said by one informant to be of the Sarakoolie tribe of Senegal.

[23] The archival source is: District Commissioner, Ronietta District (E. D.'H. Fairt-lough), *Decree Book*, Southern Province, Ronietta District, Vol. II (1905-21), pp. 191-93 (on deposit in the District Office, Moyamba.) The missionary reference is Hursh, 1918, p. 18.

[24] Important oral sources are Interviews No. 32, Taiama, Kori Chiefdom, pp. 209-10; No. 44, Taiama, pp. 274-75; No. 67, Taiama, pp. 416-19; No. 60, Waiima, Kori Chiefdom, pp. 358-60; and No. 62, Mokundi, Kori Chiefdom, p. 377.

The influence of the Wali-yu's ministry upon Islam in the chiefdom is difficult to assess. The training of the scholars lent to the development of leadership for Islam of the Mende type in outlying towns and villages. The scholars returned to become, in some cases, village leaders and are of the Mende Muslim type because they to not refrain from secret society participation. So far as his radical reforming tendencies were concerned the thrust of the Wali-yu was directed at the secret institutions at the heart of Mende society. Though he was unsuccessful in imposing the social authority of Islam as he understood it on the chiefdom, it appears that the ranks of the Mende Muslim type were swollen by the efforts of the Wali-yu. From that time until this the Mende Muslims have been vastly predominant over the Stranger Muslims in absolute numbers. Still, because the Stranger Muslims continue to fill all the leadership roles in the central mosque at Taiama they are thus far more influential in the normative developments of Islam than the Mende Muslims, while the latter resist influence that threatens the existence of their societies.

IV

We have presented considerable evidence that Mende Muslims in this chiefdom continue to understand the world from within the Mende traditional view and have subsumed selected aspects of Islam into that world view. This evidence might suggest the need for a reappraisal of the strength of Mende (and perhaps of West African) traditional institutions relative to Islamic encroachments. Trimingham appears to hold that though the traditional world view has shaped Islam to some extent in West Africa, nevertheless, Islamic culture is gradually and inevitably breaking down animist life.[25] Little suggests that Islam has largely taken over the Mende indigenous faith.[26] These assessments may be correct. Yet, additional time perspective may lead observers to the conclusion that the traditional world view has exhibited sufficient strength and flexibility so as to enable it to assimilate selected features of Islam, to include them within itself, and perhaps even to take on the appearance of Islam. But it is the nature of the understanding of man and the cosmos, not the particular practices, that is determinative and if the Mende frame of reference

---

[25] Trimingham, 1961, p. 34.
[26] Little, 1967, p. 136.

continues to provide meaning for the masses even while they use elements of Islam it is Islam itself that will have been "converted." The question is not closed by any means, at least in Kori Chiefdom, and perhaps the firm conclusions reached in years hence will come closer than our generation is able to an understanding of the complexities involved in this process of cultural interaction and attitudinal change.

In short, the patterns of Islam in Kori Chiefdom have been shaped in such a way that two distinct types of Islam have been and still are to be observed. In this dualism the type denoted as Stranger Islam has been oriented toward the Koran and Muslim culture and has maintained a certain autonomy from Mende cultural life and institutions. Stranger Muslims have played a valued role of linking the Mende agricultural consumer-producers and the modernizing forces impinging upon the chiefdom from the outside, but have not succeeded in winning large numbers of converts. Mende Islam, the second type, has won many adherents and operates within the Mende worldview as a means for the acquisition and channeling of *halei* or "force" in addition to or in some cases even in place of means heretofore possessed by Mende people. It may be inaccurate to conclude that Mende traditional religion is disintegrating before a Muslim onset. Rather, it may be that the Mende have been able to limit the influence of Islam to certain valued interposal functions between needs and the sources of satisfaction, and that Mende Islam is best to be understood as a form of Mende traditional religion with technical aspects of Islam added for practical purposes. Whether these tentative conclusions are valid and whether they can be generalized for application to other areas in West Africa awaits further testing.

CHAPTER SIX

IMPACT AND RESPONSE

Though the modernization process has not yet run its course in Sierra Leone, individual studies of it must conclude. In this chapter I will offer some final observations on the interactions of Islam, Christianity and Mende traditional religion within the general context of the impact of the West and the African response.

Dealing first with Islam, it is notable that Islam was first carried into Mendeland in the context of a trading culture with no immediate political aspirations. The Mende were the hosts to the Muslim traders from the North, and the strangers stayed on Mende terms. Likewise, the nineteenth century Muslim practitioners attached to the households of Mende chiefs were undoubtedly allowed to practice because they were thought to be so much like the familiar Mende *halemui* (practitioners in *hale*). Hence, in the nineteenth century, Islam in Mendeland offered no substantial threat to accustomed Mende modes of thought and practice.

During the twentieth century, a certain distinctive kind of Islam, called "Mende Islam" above, emerged in Kori Chiefdom. I contend that Mende Islam is best understood as customary Mende culture modified by selective additions of technical aspects of Islam. Adherents of Mende Islam continue to be involved in chiefdom politics and secret societies. Perhaps over the coming generations, Mende Islam will undergo a gradual transformation into a more normative form of Islam, as Trimingham predicts, but the continuing strength of Mende life during the past two centuries precludes any foregone conclusion on this point.

Different than Mende Islam is Stranger Islam, the normative Maliki Islam characteristic of the small trading community of Fula, Susu and Mandingo folk living in Kori Chiefdom, Like Mende Islam, but for different reasons, Stranger Islam does not threaten Mende society in practice. Stranger Islam would like to overcome the Mende secret societies and organize social and political life on the basis of the interpretation of the Koran given by elders of the mosque. But since Stranger Islam is adhered to by such a small percentage of the population, no hope exists of bringing chiefdom life into regular

Muslim forms. This was made evident in the second decade of the twentieth century when the chief of Taiama evicted the Wali-yu from the chiefdom. So normative Islam in Kori Chiefdom continues to be the practice of only a minority of persons, strangers to the central cultural and political underpinnings and institutions of the Mende majority in the chiefdom.

In this light, it would appear that the great challenge of the future for Islam is to seek to substitute Muslim law and tradition for the customary Mende ethos and law, thus achieving conciliation of Mende and Stranger Islam.

Christianity achieved significant influence in the Kpaa Mende-Bumpe areas later than Islam. Furthermore, while Islam was carried to Kori by traders and practitioners who did not threaten accustomed Mende ways, Christianity arrived on the scene firmly allied to colonialism, which, in addition to economic aims, had political and cultural goals as well that threatened Mende forms of life. The colonial impact was dramatically underlined by the British victory over the defenders of Mende sovereignty during the Hut Tax War (or *puugwei*, "White Man's War") of 1898.

Even before the *puugwei*, some Africans found missionary Christianity valuable for certain ends, but after the imposition of Christianity, in effect by force, Africans discovered that institutions maintained by the mission were extremely useful in adjusting to the impact of modernization. The constant presence and accessibility of missionaries provided opportunities from time to time to observe and practice Western manners, styles of dress and the English language. Such opportunities in general were enhanced many times over if one, or one's child, could find a place in the missionary school. Formal education under mission auspices served as a significant means of entry into professions, occupations and political careers opened up by colonialism.

Nineteenth century missionary Christianity posed a definite threat in principle to Mende life because of its opposition to secret societies and its alliance with colonial political aims in the rural areas. But the rules of missionary Christianity were gradually relaxed to accommodate the growing group of "town Christians" in the twentieth century. This group consisted of persons who had received formal schooling from the mission, spoke English, followed Western patterns of conventional life in many respects, and yet continued to defend African secret societies and political institutions. Town Christianity took form particularly after authority devolved from the American missionary to the African pastor in the 1950s, and at about this time it became apparent that Town Christianity was different than missionary Christianity in principle because it offered no significant threat to accustomed Mende institutional life. There was no form of Islam in Kori Chiefdom exactly analogous to Town Christianity. Neither Mende Islam nor Stranger Islam qualified. The "Neo-Islam" described by Trimingham is a close analogue, but Neo-Islam is nonexistent in any significant measure in Kori Chiefdom.[1]

Another distinct kind of Christianity, called Village Christianity, took form in Kori Chiefdom when large numbers of rural persons adhered to the church and adopted some aspects of Christian practice without giving up Mende beliefs or practices. The Muslim analogue is Mende Islam. In both cases, selected aspects of the universal religion were assimilated onto a Mende social base.

Village Christianity as a synthetic emergence was possible in part because of the African pragmatic stance toward *halei* and possible means of its manipulation. It was possible from the Christian side because of the strong commitment of missionaries and pastors to the universalization of their faith among the populace. For rural Mende, it came to act as an absorber of the impact of the West, allowing them sufficient identification with Christianity to satisfy the minimal demands of resident pastors and missionaries while at the same time modifying those patterns to such an extent that accustomed Mende patterns could continue. In fact, Village Christianity signified the reshaping of that religion into the mold of the Mende social style.

The twentieth century seems to have presented Christianity with two great problems in rural Sierra Leone. The first problem was to overcome the drag of its close affiliation with colonialism during the Ante-Protectorate and the early Protectorate periods. This includes the strong reliance of Christianity on formal education and its general role as an instrument of the Western-based modernization process. It especially includes the *de facto* reliance of missionaries on the force of arms during the *puugwei* as a means to establish and defend the missionary institutions, a morally dubious (even if necessary) form of defense for Christians if judged by the stated norms of the UBC.

---

[1] Cf. p. 77.

With the development of Town and Village Christianity as expressions of ongoing Mende life, the first great problem was overcome. But many problems are resolved with solutions that bring other problems in turn, and it seems so in this case. The second challenge for both Town and Village Christianity will be to overcome their apparently instrumental relationships to the Mende style of life and to achieve a stance of simultaneous involvement with, but independence from, Mende life. In other words, the second great problem for Christianity will be to solve the Christ and culture problem in such a way that a further and new creation, as yet unimagined, may emerge in rural Sierra Leone.

The traditional religion of the rural societies was diffusive, pragmatic and inwardly oriented by nature. Defeat in the *puugwei* of 1898 put the traditional religion, along with the culture from which it was so indistinguishable, on the defensive. Under conditions of defeat, military defense was necessarily abandoned in favor of selective assimilation and compromise, reminiscent of the reciprocity pattern pioneered by new rulers in the Ante-Protectorate period. The result was a synthetic social style basically African in nature.

The great question, still unresolved, is whether the Mende basis for the synthetic social style is strong enough to sustain itself indefinitely. If not, either Muslim, Christian or secular bases, or some combination of them, will be substituted as the basis for some new style of life in rural Sierra Leone.

No doubt, a markedly African cast will be apparent in whatever social style emerges in rural Sierra Leone in the near or distant future. Yet, if and as interfacing between the great world cultural areas becomes more dense, it seems certain that Islam, Christianity and modernization will all leave a permanent imprint on rural Sierra Leone.

Modernization theory has been employed as a basic framework, and has proven meritorious in many respects, for this study in comparative religious ethics. Religion, if understood as defined above, is "global" in scope in reference to any particular culture, and a study of religion thus calls for a "global" social theory.[2] Modernization theory has proven itself capable of relating persons and society and values and attitudes in the economic, political, social and cultural spheres. In this way, it facilitated a coherent, comparative, "global"

---

[2] Cf. p. 2.

study of religious interactions. Second, modernization theory is descriptive of the particular historical trend it names, and has proven useful in understanding the problems and prospects presented to African traditional religion, Christianity, and Islam within the context of that trend. Therefore, modernization theory is helpful for the comparative study of religious ethics; it helps elicit the necessary data and provides a frame of reference by which similar data from two or more cultures may be compared.

Yet, modernization theory is not useful unconditionally. As I have worked with the theory, I have found it has significant weaknesses both on its own terms and as an instrument for comparative religious ethics. The first weakness is that the emphasis of the theory is weighted toward the modern side of the equation and therefore seems to deal inadequately with the whole. For instance, a more adequately differentiated terminology has been developed for reference to the modern, as opposed to the traditional, sector. I found it necessary to define and interpret traditional society in ways not envisioned by the theory. The traditional side turned out to be stronger in its own right and to have a far greater capacity for creativity and vitality than I had been led to expect.

But the second liability is even more significant. I have found it impossible to escape the conclusion that modernization theory goes beyond value-free description to embody certain assumptions that mark it as a normative social theory.[3] That is, modernization theory not only describes how worldwide social history has progressed, but also implies how society ought to change. I will mention two respects in which modernization theory is normative. First, it assumes that history is by nature open-ended; and second, it assumes a linear concept of history. Both of these assumptions are implied in the notion that modern societies are capable of *appropriate* response to the problems that arise from the modernization process itself.[4] The word "appropriate" is normative, but remains unintelligible until one assumes a historical process embodying creativity and moving toward some end or *telos*. Such an assumption may be correct, but it should be recognized that a philosophy of history lies deep at the heart of modernization theory, and that this carries important consequences for the study of cultures.

---

[3] This aspect of modernization theory is rarely discussed by modernization theorists, but see Shils, 1963, pp. 24-26.

[4] Cf. p. 4.

To push this line one step further, it now becomes apparent that modernization theory itself has religious significance if we continue with the symbolic definition of religion advanced earlier.[5] For comparative religious ethics, this would mean that modernization theory does not offer an objective, neutral basis for comparison between religions and cultures. Use of the theory implies a stance with a religious significance of its own. The discovery of such religious implications leads one to seek broader explanations of modernization theory itself — a search which ends in metaphysics unless one draws an arbitrary line of demarcation short of the question of ultimate reality.[6]

Perhaps at this very point, Islam, Christianity and Mende traditional religion can find a new opening to the future. The opening to be suggested would by no means completely solve the problem of differences among the three religions, but might promote productive relationships between them while guaranteeing their respective integrities. The nature of religious interaction in Sierra Leone would be significantly altered from that of a triangular competition to that of a dialectic relationship between various forms of explicit religion on the one hand and the implicit religious elements of the modernization process on the other. Traditional Mende, Muslim and Christian religions could cooperate in seeking an explicitly religious understanding of the meaning of modernization, and in anticipating the emergence of a new social synthesis in post-traditional rural African society.

What this new synthesis-to-be-imagined may be is not yet clearly realized. But it will probably include these components. (1) Mende life will be irrevocably joined to an emerging global civilization, along with all other particular tribal, ethnic and cultural groups. (2) The Mende people will enrich this global civilization by virtue of maintaining their own unique social style, refined through interaction with exogenous cultural influences. (3) The examination and refinement of the Mende social style will come in part through its interaction with the prophetic and legal aspects of Christianity and Islam. (4) Christianity and Islam may yet come to be understood

---

[5] Bellah (1970, p. 206) recently said that every sociology implies a theology. That statement certainly tests out well in this case.

[6] Deats (1972, pp. 33-34) states that social science and social ethics are best held in dialetical tension, mutually critical and corrective.

as servants, not enemies, of the true health of the Mende nation. (5) The implicitly religious process of modernization may come to be acknowledged explicitly, thus making it one among equals as an option for an informing symbolic commitment. Christianity, Islam, and aspects of life associated with modernization might all come to contribute to a new historical understanding of "deep Mende."

ABREVIATIONS USED IN THIS BOOK

Abbreviated Titles of Organizations and Nations

AMA	American Missionary Association
DOA-M	District Office Archives, Moyamba
EUB	Evangelical United Brethren Church
EUBA	EUB Archives of UMC
NA	Native Administration
S.L.	Sierra Leone
SLA	Sierra Leone Government Archives
UBC	Church of the United Brethren in Christ
UMC	The United Methodist Church
WMA	Woman's Missionary Association

Abbreviated Titles of Government Officials

C.S.	Colonial Secretary
D.C.	District Commissioner
G.I.	Government Interpreter
S.A.D.	Superintendent of Aborigines Department
S.D.N.A.	Secretary of the Department of Native Affairs

Abbreviated Titles of Serials

C.M.	United Brethren in Christ, West Africa Conference. *Minutes of the Annual Sessions*
S.L.O.	*Sierra Leone Outlook*
S.L.S.	*Sierra Leone Studies*
W.E.	*Woman's Evangel*

Abbreviated Titles of Manuscript Materials

ADLB	Aborigines Department Letter Book
ADMP	Aborigines Department Minute Paper
A/NADLB	Aborigines/Native Affairs Department Letter Book
CSMP	Colonial Secretary's Minute Paper
GALB	Governor's Aborigines Letter Book
GCDSS	Governor's Confidential Despatches to the Secretary of State for the Colonies.
GILB	Government Interpreter's Letter Book
GIM	Government Interpreter's Memoranda
MP	Minute Paper
NAMP	Native Administration Minute Paper

LIST OF SOURCES

PUBLISHED SOURCES

Alldridge, T. J.
1901 *The Sherbro and its Hinterland.* London : Macmillan and Co.
Bellah, R. N. (Ed.)
1965 *Religion and Progress in Modern Asia.* New York : Free Press.
Bellah, R. N.
1970 *Beyond Belief : Essays on Religion in a Post-Traditional World.* New York :
       Harper & Row.
Best, J. Ralph.
1949 *A History of the Sierra Leone Railway, 1899-1949.* (Mimeographed.)
Deats, Paul, Jr.
1972 "The Quest for a Social Ethic." In Paul Deats, Jr. (Ed.), *Toward A Discipline
       of Social Ethics : Essays in Honor of Walter George Muelder.* Boston :
       Boston University Press, pp. 21-48.
de Hart, Julian.
1920 "Introduction to the Caulker Manuscript." *Sierra Leone Studies* o.s. IV :
       17-28.
Denzer, LaRay.
1968 "A Diary of Bai Bureh's War : Part I : February 1st-April 1st : Bai Bureh
       Holds the Initiative." *Sierra Leone Studies* n.s. 23 : 39-65.
Denzer, LaRay and Michael Crowder.
1970 "Bai Bureh and the Sierra Leone Hut Tax War of 1898." In Robert
       I. Rotberg and Ali A. Mazrui (Eds.), *Protest and Power in Black Africa.*
       New York : Oxford University Press, pp. 169-212.
Deutsch, Karl.
1961 "Social Mobilization and Political Development." *American Political Science
       Review* LV (3) : 463-514.
Domingo, G. M.
1922 "The Caulker Manuscript." *Sierra Leone Studies* o.s. IV : 1-30.
Easmon, M. C. F.
1958 "Madam Yoko, Ruler of the Mendi Confederacy." *Sierra Leone Studies*
       n.s. 11 : 165-68.
Edel, May and Abraham.
1968 *Anthropology and Ethics : The Quest for Moral Understanding.* Rev. Ed. ;
       Cleveland : Press of Case Western Reserve University.
Eisenstadt, S. N.
1965 "Social Change in African Societies South of the Sahara." *Cahier étude
       africaine* V (3) : 453-71.
1966 *Modernization : Protest and Change.* Englewood Cliffs, N. J. : Prentice-Hall,
       Inc.
Fisher, J. Humphrey.
1968 "Some Reflexions on Islam in Independent West Africa." *The Clergy
       Review* (March) : 1-13.

Fyfe, Christopher.
    1956   "European and Creole Influence in the Hinterland of Sierra Leone before
          1896." *Sierra Leone Studies* n.s. 6 : 113-23.
Fyfe, Christopher.
    1962a *A History of Sierra Leone*. London : Oxford University Press.
    1962b *A Short History of Sierra Leone*. London : Longmans, Green and Company.
Geertz, Clifford.
    1966   "Religion as a Cultural System." In Michael Banton (Ed.), *Anthropological
          Approaches to the Study of Religion*. A.S.A. Monographs 3; London :
          Tavistock Publications, Ltd., pp. 1-46.
Gibb, H. A. R. and J. H. Kramer (Eds.)
    1953   *Shorter Encyclopedia of Islam*. Leiden : E. J. Brill.
Gray, Richard.
    1968   "Problems of Historical Perspective : The Planting of Christianity in Africa
          in the Nineteenth and Twentieth Centuries." In C. G. Baëta (Ed.), *Christianity
          in Tropical Africa*. London : Oxford University Press for the International
          African Institute.
Great Britain.
    1887   Cmnd. 5236. *Further Correspondence Respecting Disturbances in the Native
          Territories Adjacent to Sierra Leone. (In Continuation of C. 4905*. London.
Great Britain, Colonial Office.
    1892   *Collection of Treaties with Native Chiefs, &c on the West Coast of Africa*
          (London, 1892), Part II, "Sierra Leone," pp. 49-294.
Great Britain, Commission of Inquiry on the Subject of the Insurrection in the Sierra
    Leone Protectorate, 1898.
    1899   Cmnd. 9391. Part I : *Report... on the... Insurrection in the Sierra Leone
          Protectorate, 1898*. Part II : *Evidence and Documents*. Edinburgh and London :
          T. and A. Constable for Her Majesty's Stationery Office.
Groenendyke, Ellen.
    1901   "Glorious Eighth of July." *Woman's Evangel* XX (10) : 156.
    1921   "Three Early African Experiences." *The Evangel* XL (7-8) : 201-03.
Gustafson, James M.
    1972   "The Relevance of Historical Understanding." In Paul Deats, Jr. (Ed.),
          *Toward a Discipline of Social Ethics : Essays in Honor of Walter George
          Muelder*. Boston : Boston University Press, pp. 49-70.
Hallowell, Thomas F.
    1928   "Autobiography." (Typescript.)
Harford, Mrs. L. R.
    1934   "Reminiscences of a Long Life." *The Evangel* LII (5) : 149-50.
Hargreaves, J. D.
    1954   "The Evolution of the Native Affairs Department." *Sierra Leone Studies*
          n.s. 3 : 168-84.
Hirst, Elizabeth.
    1957   "An Attempt at Reconstructing the History of the Loko [*sic*] People from
          about 1790 to the Present Day." *Sierra Leone Studies* n.s. 9 : 26-39.
Hodgkin, Thomas.
    1957   *Nationalism in Colonial Africa*. New York : New York University Press.

Hopewell, James Franklin.
   1958   "Muslim Penetration into French Guinea, Sierra Leone, and Liberia before
          1850." Unpublished Ph.D. dissertation, Columbia University.
Hough, Mrs. S. S.
   1958   *Faith that Achieved : A History of the Women's Missionary Association
          of the Church of the United Brethren in Christ, 1872-1946.* [Dayton, Ohio:]
          Women's Society of World Service of the Evangelical United Brethren
          Church.
Houtart, François.
   1972   "The Demand for Economic Justice : Southern Africa and the Portuguese
          Colonies." In Paul Deats, Jr. (Ed.), *Toward a Discipline of Social Ethics :
          Essays in Honor of Walter George Muelder.* Boston : Boston University
          Press, 1972, pp. 194-217.
Hursh, E. M.
   1918   "At the Forks of the Road." *Evangel* XXXVII (1) : 16-20.
Hutchinson, Bertram.
   1957   "Some Social Consequences of Nineteenth Century Missionary Activity
          among the South African Bantu." *Africa* XXVII (2) : 160-77.
Kilson, Martin.
   1966   *Political Change in a West African State : A Study of the Modernization
          Process in Sierra Leone.* Cambridge, Mass. : Harvard University Press.
King, J. R.
   1899   "Report to the Board of Managers," WMA, May 17, 1899. *Woman's Evangel*
          XVIII (6) : 94.
[Kokoya-] Daugherty, S. F.
   1932   "Life Sketch of S. F. Daugherty." *Sierra Leone Outlook* XXIII (9) : 7.
Leader, Charles.
   1936   "Work at Taiama [sic] Station." *The Evangel* LV (3) : 77-80.
Little, Kenneth.
   1946   "A Moslem 'Missionary' in Mendeland." *Man* XLVI (102) : 111-13.
   1954   "The Mende of Sierra Leone." In Daryll Forde (Ed.), *African Worlds.*
          London : Oxford University Press for the International African Institute,
          pp. 111-37.
   1967   *The Mende of Sierra Leone : A West African People in Transition.* Rev. ed. ;
          London : Routledge & Kegan Paul.
McCulloch, M.
   1964   *Peoples of Sierra Leone*, Western Africa, Part II of *Ethnographic Survey
          of Africa*, (Ed.) Daryll Forde. Reprinted with supplementary bibliography ;
          London and Watford : Stone & Cox, Ltd. for the International African
          Institute.
McGrew, L. A.
   1898   Letter of February 25, 1898 in *Woman's Evangel* XVII (6) : 103.
MacIver, R. N.
   1965   *The Web of Government.* Rev. ed. ; New York : Free Press.
Muelder, Walter G.
   1966   *Moral Law in Christian Social Ethics.* Richmond : John Knox Press.
Niebuhr, H. Richard.
   1963   *The Responsible Self : An Essay in Christian Moral Philosophy.* New York :
          Harper & Row, Publishers.

Ojabemi, Ade.
    1966 "The Founding of Kori Chiefdom." Njala, Sierra Leone : Njala University
          College. (Mimeographed.)
Olson, Gilbert W.
    1969 *Church Growth in Sierra Leone.* Grand Rapids : William B. Eerdmans
          Publishing Company.
Porter, Arthur T.
    1963 *Creoledom — A Study of the Development of Freetown Society.* London :
          Oxford University Press.
Redfield, Robert.
    1968 *The Primitive World and its Transformations.* Harmondsworth : Penguin
          Books.
Reeck, Darrell L.
    1968 "Church Renewal and Social Reconstruction : A Missionary Bishop Shows
          the Way." *World Outlook* (May) : 34-35.
    1971 See List of Sources — Personal Interviews.
Reeck, Darrell and John H. Ness.
    1969 "Research Notes : United Methodist Archival Materials Relative to the
          History of Sierra Leone." *Sierra Leone Bulletin of Religion* XI : 45-51.
    1972 "Research Notes : Sierra Leone Holdings in United Methodist Archives."
          Methodist History X (3) : 48-53.
Renner, S. M.
    1966 "History of the United Brethren Mission in Sierra Leone." (Typescript.)
Riddell, J. Barry.
    1970 *The Spatial Dynamics of Modernization in Sierra Leone : Structure, Diffusion,
          and Response.* Evanston : Northwestern University Press.
Rodney, Walter.
    1967 "A Reconsideration of the Mane Invasions of Sierra Leone." *Journal of
          African History* VIII (2) : 219-46.
Rotberg, Robert I.
    1964 "Missionaries as Chiefs and Entrepreneurs : Northern Rhodesia, 1882-1924."
          In Jeffrey Butler (Ed.), *Boston University Papers in African History,*
          Volume I. Boston : Boston University Press, pp. 196-215.
Shils, Edward.
    1963 "On the Comparative Study of New States." In Clifford Geertz (Ed.),
          Old Societies and New States. New York : Free Press of Glencoe : 1-26.
Sierra Leone, Administrator.
    1886 *Despatch from the Administrator-in-Chief Enclosing Information Regarding
          the Different Districts and Tribes of Sierra Leone and Its Vicinity.* Sierra
          Leone : Colonial Office.
Singer, Milton.
    1971 "Beyond Tradition and Modernity in Madras." *Comparative Studies in Society
          and History* XIII (2) : 160-95.
Smart, J. K.
    1932 "Short Life Sketch of Reverend J. K. Smart." *Sierra Leone Outlook* XXIII
          (1) : 9-11.
Smurl, Joseph.
    1972 *Religious Ethics : A Systems Approach.* Englewood Cliffs, N. J. : Prentice-
          Hall, Inc.

Trimingham, John Spencer.
1961   *Islam in West Africa.* 2nd Printing; London : Oxford University Press.
1966   "Islam and Secular Nationalism in Africa." *The Muslim World* LVI (4): 303-07.
Trimingham, John Spencer and Christopher Fyfe.
1960   "Early Expansion of Islam in Sierra Leone." *Sierra Leone Bulletin of Religion* II (2) : 33-39.
Troeltsch, Ernst.
1971   *The Absoluteness of Christianity and the History of Religions.* Trans. David Reid. Richmond : John Knox Press.
UBC, West African Conference.
1899   "Report of the Superintendent." *Minutes of the Nineteenth Annual Session, 1899.* Dayton, Ohio : United Brethren Publishing House.
Warner, I. D.
1954   "The Story of a Successful Church in Africa." *The Telescope-Messenger* (April 3) : 9-10.
Williams, T. Mylar-Bumpeh.
c. 1930   "A Brief Biography of Sorie Kessebeh : Warrior and King of Rotifunk-Bumpeh Chiefdom." (Typescript.)
Witt, Mrs. B. F.
1893   "Nineteenth Annual Report of the Corresponding Secretary of the WMA." *Woman's Evangel* XII (6) : 94.
1897   "Annual Report of the Corresponding Secretary," WMA, Lisbon, Iowa, May 12, 1897, *Woman's Evangel* XVI (6) : 91.
1898   "Annual Report of the Corresponding Secretary to the Board," WMA, May 18, 1898, *Woman's Evangel* XVII (6) : 95-96.
Woman's Missionary Association, African Committee.
1885   "Report of the African Committee." *Woman's Evangel* IV (5) : 83.
Yinger, J. Milton.
1970   *The Scientific Study of Religion.* New York : Macmillan Company.

ARCHIVAL SOURCES

(Note : all entries are from SLA unless otherwise noted)
Aborigines Department File, 1881. (1 file.)
Aborigines Department Letter Book, 1882-90. (6 volumes.)
Aborigines Department Minute Papers, 1887-90. (10 boxes, assorted loose papers.)
Aborigines/Native Affairs Department Letter Book, 1890-91. (1 volume.)
Colonial Secretariat Minute Papers, Nos. 1-500, 1880. (1 box.)
Colonial Secretary's Office, Letters Received, 1850-69. (1 file.)
Confidential Aborigines/Native Affairs Department Letter Book, 1889-98. (1 volume.)
Confidential Despatches from the Governor of Sierra Leone to the Secretary of State for the Colonies, 1907, 1911, 1912. (3 book files.)
Despatches from the Governor of Sierra Leone to the Secretary of State for the Colonies, 1900, 1902, 1903, 1907, 1909. (9 volumes, 2 bundles.)
District Commissioner, Ronietta, Minute Papers, 1916. (1 bundle.)
Government Interpreter's Letter Book, 1876-1889. (10 volumes.)
Government Interpreter's Memoranda, 1873-1878. (2 volumes.)

Governor's Aborigines Letter Book, 1878-1882. (1 volume.)
Governor's Despatches to the Secretary of State, 1909. (1 bundle.)
Native Affairs Department Letter Book, 1891-1899. (6 volumes.)
Ronietta District Decree Book, Vol. II, 1907-21. (1 volume.) DOA-M.
Ronietta District Intelligence Diary, 1900-21. (1 volume.) DOA-M.

PERSONAL INTERVIEWS

Reeck, Darrell L.
  1971 "Oral Data Regarding the History of the Process of Modernization and
     Related Mission Influences in Sierra Leone, Gathered in 1968-69." (Type-
     script.) Copies of this collection of 148 interviews are available to scholars
     at : Oral Data Archives of the African Studies Association, Indiana Univer-
     sity; Institute of African Studies, Fourah Bay College, University of Sierra
     Leone; Mugar Memorial Library African Studies Collection, Boston Univer-
     sity; and the EUB Archives of The United Methodist Church, Dayton, Ohio.